Faculty of Education, University of Western Ontario
THE CANADIAN CURRICULUM: A PERSONAL VIEW, *Barrow*

By the same author:

Sparta
Athenian Democracy
Plato and Education
Plato, Utilitarianism and Education
Plato: Apology. Introduction and Commentary
Greek and Roman Education
Introduction to Philosophy of Education
(with R. Woods)
Common Sense and the Curriculum
Moral Philosophy for Education
Radical Education

The Canadian Curriculum: A Personal View

Robin Barrow

Faculty of Education
University of Western Ontario
London, Ontario

Editorial Assistants: Gwyneth Williams, David Jowett and Judson Purdy

ISBN 0-920354-04-1
Printed and bound in Canada.

For Geoff Milburn, who gets things done, and for Joan, Ann and Karen who put up with him doing them, this essay, a small gesture of gratitude that one of them will read.

ACKNOWLEDGEMENTS

I should like to express my special thanks to Shirley Skinner. I have written many books, but never had the privilege of working with so good a secretary. I am also indebted to Gwyneth Williams, no matter how she spells her name, for her meticulous editing.

CONTENTS

CHAPTER 1

On Writing Books About the Curriculum

1.1 A great deal of the disillusion that some people feel with books about education appears to arise from a failure to perceive the nature and purpose of the books in question. If you are looking for examples of lesson plans for the history teacher, you will obviously be disappointed in a book which questions the value of teaching history at all. If you wish to reflect upon the question of how current curriculum practice originated, you will be irritated by books on curriculum that treat current practice as the natural order of events. In these opening paragraphs (1.1—1.10) I shall therefore attempt to outline the nature, purpose, point and limitations of this essay.

1.2 If there were a Trades Description Act relating to education, many of us would face prosecution. There is an alarming discrepancy between what we claim to be teaching or teaching for and what we are actually doing. From kindergarten through to the faculties of education, lesson plans, course descriptions, Ministry guidelines and even legally binding statutes are circulated which are seriously misleading: we do not deliver the goods we promise. Sometimes this is a matter of falling short of our ideals. Sometimes it is a matter of being ensnared by daunting practical difficulties. But very often it is a case of our doing things that are inappropriate to our stated end or aims, because we do not really understand what is involved in those ends or aims, and therefore do not know what would be appropriate to them. Thus we get courses at college level which claim to teach people how to teach children to be critical thinkers, but fail, essentially because it is not clear what constitutes 'critical thinking'. Courses in formal logic may be advertised on the grounds that they have some important link with sound reasoning, although there is no agreement on what the nature of the link between formal logic and everyday reasoning may be. At the high school level a particular course in social studies may be justified in terms of its contribution to developing the democratic spirit. But what *is* the democratic spirit and what sort of thing does develop it? All too often that kind of question has not been satisfactorily answered or even examined. At the elementary or junior level the situation is not necessarily any different: what is actually going on is often referred to some aim or set of aims (e.g., 'the realization of the self', 'the development of creativity', 'the growth of the whole child'). But those aims themselves remain unexamined, obscure and therefore no real guide or yardstick to our practice.

In a sentence: our practice is impeded by the fact that we run away from the task of properly thinking things through. We seem reluctant to face up to the importance and significance of the question 'why' in education, despite the fact that it must precede and is ultimately more crucial than the 'how' question on which we spend so much more time. Many teachers seem quite contented to take course after course on how to teach, say, drama, without giving any thought at all to the questions of what studying drama actually involves or why anybody should use limited curriculum time in doing it. But coherent talk about how we should teach presupposes some view about why we are doing whatever we try to do. A change in our reasons for doing something (the 'why') may necessitate a change in how we do it. A slight change in how we do something may make a nonsense of the idea that our original reasons for doing it are being served. The question 'why' comes first: it is only in the light of specific answers to the question 'why do this?' that it can become true that this is precisely what we should do and that we should do it in this way rather than that. Yet it seems difficult to dissent from the conclusion of Hall and Carlton that "the schools [in Ontario] have accumulated an awesome range of objectives . . . [but] there has been no systematic debate as to the appropriateness of school objectives" or their real meaning.[1]

1.3 The above remarks clearly herald some kind of theoretical or abstract discussion. I had better clarify therefore, what I mean by educational theory. First, it is not comparable to scientific theory by which phrase we refer to an accredited body of interrelated ideas within the domain of science. There might conceivably one day be a body of educational theory in that sense, but there certainly isn't at the moment. Education as an area of study is too diffuse, there is too little consensus and too little is known for certain, to allow us to claim that educational theory may be regarded as parallel to scientific theory. At the present time one must take the phrase educational theory to mean 'a body of loosely connected observations about education arrived at through various constituent disciplines'. Educational theory is made up of historical insights and explanations, more or less well researched hypotheses about child psychology, sociological data and philosophical inquiry. To engage in educational theory is not therefore to embrace a particular discipline or to pursue one particular kind of question. Nor is it to theorize in the sense of idly dream or speculate without concern for hard evidence. It is to think things through systematically with particular reference to such pertinent data (historical, psychological or whatever) as there may be. Ideally, educational theory presupposes competence in the various constituent disciplines (so that the claims fed in can themselves be checked and challenged), and it transcends them (so that specifically educational claims are not made on the basis of, say, a particular historical view or psychological hypothesis alone).

1.4 In this sense of theory there is obviously no gulf between theory and practice. Broadly speaking 'theory' is equivalent to 'informed thought' and 'practice' to 'action'. The relationship between the two is therefore very close. Certainly one *can* act without thought, which is to say engage in practice without studying theory, and indeed most of the time we do. One *can* also think about something without carrying it through in action or think in defiance of what is realistic or practical. But to think about something in a way that turns out to be impractical is to engage in poor theorizing. The fact that very often theorizing about education is poor does not show that theory as such is futile or impractical; it just shows that it needs to be done better. Again, the fact that theory and practice can be, and very often are, divorced shows only that. It does not show that they cannot or should not be related. The plain truth is that thinking about one's actions enables one to understand, plan and control. At worst it allows one to explain to others what one is doing and at best it will enable one to see and find ways of modifying and improving what one is doing. There may be times when it would be foolish to make practice wait on theory, but, generally, the man who says "I'm a practical man myself; I've no time for theory" is telling us that he likes to do what he has grown into the habit of doing and doesn't like to ask himself whether there's good reason for him to be doing it. A teaching force made up of people like that is surely to be avoided if possible.

There is no logical gap, then, between theory and practice in my sense of the terms. The distinction that does need to be made is between good and bad thinking, between appropriate or sound and inappropriate or unsound theory. But there is always a need for sound theory.

1.5 An essay in curriculum theory involves an attempt to think curriculum matters through from the beginning in a systematic way. It must to some extent be abstract and general because, if the whole issue is really being thought through, questions such as "Why have a curriculum at all?" and "What is education supposed to be about?" have to be faced. They just happen to be rather general and abstract questions. One could insist on confining one's theorizing to the concrete and particular (e.g., "What shall I teach Johnny during second class tomorrow?"), but that would be somewhat dull by comparison, of little interest to people other than Johnny and oneself, and quite arbitrary, unless one answered the particular question in the light of answers to the more general questions. What it would be sensible to teach Johnny during second class tomorrow depends, amongst other things, on what you think teachers should be trying to do for children in schools, what children of Johnny's age and background are like in various respects, and what methods do achieve the results you hope for. If you haven't thought about those questions—well, poor Johnny, since you will opt to treat him in a particular way out of habit, under orders or at random.

1.6 If we agree to think things through systematically, what sort of things are we to think about? Essentially three: meaning, coherence and the validity of empirical claims.

i) *Meaning.* Sometimes if we scrutinize the meaning of key terms in educational claims, hypotheses or arguments, we obviate the need for any further empirical study. Take, for example, this sentence: "The economy of the 'discovery' method is now being questioned . . . [the] emphasis on discovery displaced . . . the use of 'drill' . . . [so there were a number of students in junior high school] who had never learned multiplication tables."[2] To that, written in 1977, one might add many other things that people are 'discovering' now, such as that 'discovery learning' suits some subject areas better than others and some children better than others. But the immediate point is that these kinds of qualifications to the value and use of 'discovery' learning need not have awaited the conclusion of a lengthy period of experience or empirical research. They could have been anticipated by mere dispassionate reflection on precisely what 'discovery' learning meant or was supposed to involve and be suited to. That such conclusions *could have been* anticipated is shown by the fact that they *were* amongst a few educationalists.[3]

ii) *Coherence.* Assuming we have a clear understanding of the key terms employed in educational discussions, we next need to think about whether proposals, hypotheses, claims and such like are coherent. Do they make sense, avoid internal contradiction, add up, avoid fallacious steps, and are they suited to our (hopefully now clearly articulated) aims? The need to check out that sort of question does not, incidentally, mean that we need to study logic. We need to be logical and to make sure that our reasoning about education is logical, but that is not the same thing as, nor does it necessarily require, studying logic.

iii) *Validity of empirical claims.* Empirical data is to educational theory rather as bricks are to the architect. In designing his house, the architect has to take account of what bricks are and whether they are available. His theoretical plan will be useless if it turns out that there are no bricks of the sort he requires. In the same way, coherent thinking about education obviously depends on getting the facts straight. But there the similarity ends. When all is said and done, bricks are few in kind and their essential properties are well known to architects. Facts and alleged facts relating to education are all over the place and so different that they sometimes appear to contradict each other. We certainly need to know about and take account of the findings of empirical research. But we also need to be a great deal more careful about accepting and putting our full trust in such findings than some educationalists have been. There is a depressing lack of correlation between the number of things that we actually know for certain and the number of times the phrase 'it is a well know fact that . . .' is encountered in discussion about education. (Compare 'it is a proven fact that . . .', which seems for some people to be synonymous with 'this is something that somebody tried to establish empirically'.) The fiasco over the claims made for intelligence earlier in this century, and the heated debate that still continues over the question of what part genetic endowment plays in intelligence, should be enough to warn us that we cannot just read off the results of experiment and research relating to matters like creativity, moral development and learning. We need understanding of the limitations of the research involved and the conceptual framework within which it operates. We must break the almost subconscious identification of the empirical with the clear and straightforward. Competent empiricists know this. Educationalists as a whole (administrators, professors, teachers) do not. They tend to measure the certainty of a claim by reference to the way it was derived, so that, in a crazy tipsy-topsy way, the quite inviolable logical truth that 'all bachelors are unmarried' seems less of a 'hard fact' than the dubious claim that 'most of them aren't very happy', arrived at as a result of distributing a questionnaire amongst some of them.

1.7 Besides stressing the value of thinking things through, it would be appropriate at this point for me to give notice of my stand against originality. Educational literature is increasingly dominated by a concern for originality rather than clarity and good reason. One might speculate on the reasons for this, which must surely include career considerations that lead us to write papers (like this one?) and attend conferences we could all do without. But whatever the cause, it is important to recognize that we are reaching a stage where to say of a colleague's work "it's very clear and I agree with it, of course, but it isn't very original" is to praise it with not very faint damn. The academic world is becoming cut-throat and competitive, and consequently few people dare to 'waste' precious time writing things that are straightforward, clear and, once spelt out in this way, obvious. But that is precisely what we need in education: the articulation of some clear and convincing reasons, culled from or prompted by research in various disciplines, in a straightforward way. What does it matter if "Aristotle already said that" or "that's Bruner's theory"? What matters is that if it is true it should be widely disseminated now in terms that people can understand. It is arguable that the last thing we need at this point in time is some educational theorist of genius: we just aren't ready to entertain and make good use of him.

Many considerations prompt the above paragraph, but I will cite just one: the graduate student in Ontario who, after reading my *Common Sense and the Curriculum*[4] (in which, after three quarters of the book has been devoted to weighing arguments, I draw conclusions about the content of the curriculum), remarked sourly "So what's new? What you propose is more or less what we do." Very possibly, but there is no merit in proposing something different for the sake of it. And in a world where what does go on is frequently imposed from without or for bad reasons, and where what goes on could at any time be changed, there is a lot of merit in trying to explicate and understand such reasons as there may be for and against doing what we are doing. In other words, my concern there (as ironically enough I actually said on p. 163) was not to be original for the sake of it, but to be precise and thoughtful about the whole question of education and the curriculum, and see where the argument led me. If it leads me to defend the current Ontario curriculum, which as a matter of fact it didn't, well and good. The question is whether what is said is reasonable, not whether it is amazing. I make no claims to originality or erudition in this essay either. I merely argue for certain specific things that are either not happening or, if they are, look none too safe.

1.8 I should add a word about my unusual position as an outsider. Since I have only spent one year in Canada, I naturally do not intend to make any attempt to write about Canadian schools or the educational systems as they are in the various provinces. Rather I shall begin the task of thinking things through, assuming the context of any Western industrialized state. The sorts of educational issues and argument I am concerned with, though entirely pertinent to Canada, do not presuppose any intimate knowledge of, say, the school situation in British Columbia. (Where there do seem to be features that are both important and peculiar to Canada—for example, the existence of a French and English speaking community side by side—they are taken account of and my proposals modified accordingly.) For purposes of comparison and the specific illustration of general points, however, I do make reference to the last ten years in the province of Ontario, as well as sometimes drawing attention to British practice. Possibly, when I make such references, I will betray the limitations of my knowledge about Canada. Hopefully, by way of compensation for any such deficiency, the fact that I am approaching the matter from the outside will allow me to be less bound by cultural assumptions, less inclined to let sleeping dogs lie, less respectful and more candid in my criticism than the insider is prone to be. I have certainly come to recognize that, thinking and speaking in a Canadian context, I am far more open-minded than I am when thinking in the context of education in Britain. (For example, however rational I may attempt to be, I have deep-rooted feelings and assumptions about things like the private school system in Britain, whereas in the Canadian context I have neither prior assumptions nor particular concerns about private education.) Nonetheless the reader may care to know that it *has* entered my head that I am being rather presumptuous in writing a book in Canada, about Canada, for Canadians. But I let the thought pass out again. There is not yet a very clear or long standing tradition of educational theory in Canada. So, encouraged by the generous reception accorded to other outsiders, I humbly submit this essay, which, for the most part, consists of arguments, proposals and suggestions that are essentially supra-cultural and supra-national, being derived from reflection on what schooling and education ought ideally to involve.

1.9 I shall put forward the following thesis: there is a progressive tradition in the educational thought of the Western world which has done considerable damage to the quality of such thought by its refusal to think things through carefully (chapter 2). There is also a radical tradition which, by contrast, needs to be taken very seriously, particularly where its criticism of our assumptions and practices in respect of upbringing are concerned. However, although the radical tradition has been consistently more perceptive and useful than the progressive tradition, it too has made bad mistakes and failed to think things through at times—nowhere more so than when it comes to proffered solutions to the problems diagnosed (chapter 3).

From that base I go on to argue for the principle of a common core compulsory curriculum, and then for a specific content for such a curriculum in the elementary and high school. I suggest that my proposals would bring the radical goals significantly nearer achievement than would radical proposals such as deschooling (chapter 4). Following the outline of my curriculum, I make some reference to the curricula in Britain and Ontario for comparative purposes. That task involves an important aside on more specific questions such as what is meant by 'communication', whether the study of Canadiana is an appropriate way to inspire a sense of identity, what history is supposed to be good for and what is meant by the study of English. Those questions in turn direct the essay towards questions about values education, evaluation and models of teaching (chapter 5). Reference to models of teaching leads me into the final chapter on teacher preparation—a crucial issue, of course, and one that ultimately takes us right back to the beginning: what is education supposed to be about and what should we try to achieve through the schools (chapter 6)?

1.10 Finally, since everything must have its beginning, I should make it clear at the outset that everything I say is premissed on the assumption (nominally shared by the radicals and the progressives) that ideally we would like to see a thriving community of happy, autonomous and democratic citizens, and that we believe the school system can and should contribute to that end. I shall have more to say on that assumption in chapter 4, but it is important that it should be borne in mind throughout.

Notes

1. Oswald Hall and Richard Carlton, *Basic Skills at School and Work*, The Study of Albertown an Ontario Community. Toronto: Ontario Economic Council, Occasional Paper 1, 1977, p. 273.
2. Ibid., p. 65.
3. See, for example, R. F. Dearden, "Instruction and Learning by Discovery" in R. S. Peters (ed.), *The Concept of Education*, London: Routledge and Kegan Paul, 1967, p. 135 or R. G. Woods and R. Barrow, *An Introduction to the Philosophy of Education*, London: Methuen, 1975, ch. 7.
4. Robin Barrow, *Common Sense and the Curriculum*, London: George Allen and Unwin Ltd., 1976.

CHAPTER 2

The Progressive Tradition

2.1 The purposes of this chapter are: to draw attention to a progressive tradition in educational thought which is to be distinguished from the radical tradition considered in the next chapter (2.1—2.2), to instance a document in the progressive tradition and a vivid example of not thinking things through, namely Ontario's Hall-Dennis report (2.3—2.4), and to note some of the far-reaching consequences of that report (2.5—2.6).

Both the radical and the progressive tradition have consistently wanted changes from current practice. What I mean by a radical is one who wants change going to the heart of the matter or one who favours root and branch change.[1] As a consequence the radical is almost always concerned with changes in aims as well as means, whereas the progressive is often concerned only with new ways to achieve standard goals. The progressive tends to be methodologically orientated and the tradition is closely associated with concepts such as creativity, self-realization, growth, freedom, happiness, and discovery—concepts it will be noted that are all both emotive and obscure. To be against happiness or creativity is rather like being against motherhood. But what happiness or creativity actually are and hence what we should actually *do* if we wish to encourage and promote them are matters generally left shrouded in mystery. The radical tradition too pays lip service to some of those ideals, particularly freedom and happiness, but whereas the progressive educational tradition has stressed the immediate happiness of the child and his personal freedom to do as he wants (usually claiming some link between such conditions of growth and the development of a healthy, satisfied and social adult), the radical tradition has been more concerned with the general well-being of people in society and with social freedom. In fact one of the key distinguishing features between the two is that it is characteristic of the radicals to be very politically minded: they emphasize the interplay between school and society and are equally concerned to change society and the schools, while the progressives at most hope to improve society by more effective education.[2] The progressives tend to be democratic, whilst the radicals could be more properly described as individualistic, even at times faintly anarchic. At bottom the progressives think only in terms of a world of happy children, whereas the radicals think in terms of a better world, which they interpret as a freer world.

These distinctions are not, of course, very clear cut and they are even less so in practice. Rousseau, for instance, has often been classed as a progressive, although as I have argued elsewhere, he should really be seen as a particularly tough-minded and uncompromising radical.[3] A.S. Neill, the inspiration and founder of the English school Summerhill, is likewise sometimes classed as one, sometimes the other. (Probably he should be classified as a progressive.) Nonetheless, it is possible to indicate in broad terms where some prominent educationalists belong. Paul Goodman, the author of *Compulsory Miseducation*, Ivan Illich and Everett Reimer, two advocates of deschooling, and Paulo Freire, who combines a quasi-Marxist framework with a practical programme for literacy, are evidently radicals. Stretching the term a bit, Neil Postman and Charles Weingartner, authors of *Teaching as a Subversive Activity*, may also be so classified. On the other hand John Dewey, John Holt in his early writings, William Kilpatrick, Maria Montessori and Bertrand Russell in his school practice, if not in all of his various writings, should be regarded as progressives.

2.2 The progressive tradition, though full of good intentions, has produced a remarkable quantity of vapid and poor educational theory, essentially because of its no less remarkable inability or refusal to think things through. Dewey's notorious failure to explicate the meaning of the convenient term 'growth' that he uses to cover every emergency is a case in point. (E.g., "Education is all one with growth," "growing is life," "to the growth of the child all studies are subservient." What do such remarks mean? What is he talking about?[4]) Neill's vague and inconsistent pronouncements on freedom and happiness are another. (E.g., "The child should not do anything until he comes to the opinion—his own opinion—that it should be done." Yet, Neill points out, at Summerhill "a child is *not* allowed to do as he pleases." "The aim of life is happiness." "I have never seen acne on the face of a happy and free adolescent."[5]) The writing of such men certainly conveys their attitudes, but what it consistently fails to do is to explicate its key terms and to offer a clear and coherent argument for its views. It thus places those views beyond the reach of rational assessment. But for a more up-to-date example we can turn nearer to home and refer to the Report of the Provincial Committee on Aims and Objectives of Education in the Schools of Ontario. This was published in 1968 under the title *Living and Learning* and will hereafter be referred to as the Hall-Dennis report after the names of its co-chairmen.[6]

2.3 A recent study plausibly suggests that the progressive innovations of the sixties in Ontario schools were a response to various cultural phenomena such as the explosion of knowledge, the increasingly voracious appetite of the media, more insistent calls for democratization and greater effective democratic participation throughout society.[7] The educational innovations, and the proposals that led to them, are seen as to some extent culturally determined, rather than forward looking ideas that anticipated and created the future. Such a view would certainly help to explain certain features of the Hall-Dennis report which more than any other single document successfully promoted the ideas in question. It would explain how a committee, containing few members who had had prolonged widespread experience of education or devoted serious attention to studying it, nonetheless came up with a superficially plausible rhetoric. It would explain the particular tenor of their remarks. It would explain the interesting similarities between this report and the Plowden report which came out at the same time in Britain.[8] Above all it would explain how vague and ill-thought-out slogans could be taken seriously, revered as panaceas, and adopted: the catch-phrases, the rhetoric, the style, the optimism and enthusiasm suited the mood of the people.

2.4 But, if the report was a product of its time, its shortcomings are not exclusive to any particular time and place. I do not want to beat a duck long since dead in critical estimation, especially since it now looks as if it is at last lame in public estimation as well.[9] So far as the substance of the report goes there is little to add to Daly's destructive, but substantially correct critique (though it is a pity that he reverts to the same kind of emotionalism that he condemns) and other mature reflections such as those collected under Crittenden's editorship.[10] What I do want to do is re-emphasize what was essentially wrong with the report. It was thoroughly bad not because it made deplorable suggestions or poor recommendations, which it may or may not have done, but because it was so badly presented. It is ironic that it appears to live in the public memory as at any rate a thing of beauty: an official document that was strikingly and attractively produced. Yes, but the usual price for gearing things to the popular market had to be paid. A determined effort is made to package the product, to stress appearance rather than substance, to *make* the medium the message. Thus the slogan replaces the more cautious and accurate statement; the image seizes the mind and precludes qualification; the emotional response ousts reasoned and precise deliberation about the nature, suitability and practicality of the proposals. It was badly presented in the sense that it set up ill-defined goals and proposed to achieve them by spreading enthusiasm and faith. In 1969 the then Minister of Education for Ontario complimented the report for its concern with educational aims. "I think," he said, "the philosophical attempt to define the aims and objectives of education in this Province really has been perhaps the most significant accomplishment of the Committee itself."[11] But it is precisely the fact that the Committee made no adequate attempt to *define* their aims and objectives that is to be held against it. It makes some attempt to *state*, in places one might say *sketch* its aims, but it did not clarify them or think them through.

Consequently to this day we do not know what was meant by phrases such as 'education for adaptability to a changing world' or 'dynamic learning'. It is not that anyone thinks people should *not* be able to adapt to a changing world or that anyone wants to argue that learning should be *un*dynamic. (It is the very fact that nobody would want to assert the opposite that shows such phrases up for the empty catch-phrases they are.) Nor is it a question of the phrases being incomprehensible in a literal sense. The trouble is that we are not being told anything specific, we are not being given anything we can get our teeth into, when we are told that learning should be dynamic. It is on a par with saying that love should be deep. To talk of 'adaptability to a changing world' is to remain on the level of the cliché and the platitude. It is rather as if an architect competing for the job of designing a new city were to refuse to go beyond saying that in his view it should be both beautiful and practical. The report emphasizes that for the committee "children are the focus of attention" (p. 5), but so they always were even for a schoolmaster like Dickens' Mr. Gradgrind. The difference lies not in whether one sees children as central to the enterprise of education or not, but in *how* one sees them and *how* one understands education, about neither of which the report is very illuminating.

Progressive rhetoric is particularly well-exemplified in the chapter portentously entitled "The Truth Shall Make You Free." The message that we have to get across to children, we are told, is that "The underlying aim of education is to further man's unending search for truth. Once he possesses the means to truth, all else is within his grasp. Wisdom and understanding, sensitivity, compassion, and responsibility, as well as intellectual honesty and personal integrity, will be his guides in adolescence and his companions in maturity" (p. 9). One is inclined to retort that one of the aims of education should be to stop people mouthing such pretentious emptiness. That paragraph effectively tells us nothing. It is simply a list of the most obvious high-sounding words in the language, no attempt being made here or elsewhere in the report to examine and reflect on the ideas or concepts that lie behind the words. The mere assertion that we should develop sensitivity is of no help to anyone. What is needed is a penetrating discourse on sensitivity: What characterizes it? How is it to be distinguished from the sentimental? How can I recognize it? How can I cultivate it in myself and others? Where the report does attempt to become specific and practical it becomes a list of fiats and quite unsupported claims such as that we must have a "more relaxed teacher-pupil relationship which will encourage discussion, inquiry, and experimentation, and enhance the dignity of the individual" (p. 14). (The English of the report is so often very poor that it is difficult to be certain whether there should really be a comma after 'relationship' or not. In other words it is unclear whether the committee thought that more relaxed relationships would as a matter of fact encourage discussions, etc., or whether they are asking for relaxed relationships that do, as opposed to relaxed relationships that don't. If the latter, then they forgot to give any reason for wanting relaxed relationships that do rather than more formal relationships that do. If the former, they forgot the comma.) Sometimes it resorts to the by now sadly familiar use of the empty platitude: "the atmosphere within the classroom must be positive and encouraging" (p. 14). Well, of course, it must. Who on earth would argue that it should be negative and discouraging? The question is what counts as being positive. Who is to define it and in relation to what? Encouraging what? Absolutely anything? Sometimes the argument becomes misleading in its shoddiness. To say that "learning . . . is a personal matter" (p. 49) is of course true in the sense that it cannot be done for one. But to conclude from that observation that it must be wrong to structure learning or to treat all children as alike from time to time and in some respects, and that each child must proceed entirely as he and chance dictate is fallacious. Here incidentally, in the chapter "The Learning Experience," is an example of another stylistic tendency of progressive literature: the tendency to see complex issues in terms of a simple polarization between black and white. The abridged edition, put out by the Ontario Teachers' Federation, remarks that "this Report emphasizes a dynamic child-centred theory of learning rather than the stimulus-response and conditioning approach"[12] as if one had no choice but to opt for one or the other. The report itself is actually slightly more cautious at this juncture, but the same polarization is evident, as it is even more clearly in sentences like this: "The lock-step structure of past times must give way to a system in which the child will progress from year to year . . . without the hazards and frustrations of failure" (p. 14).

One might reasonably add that, as James Paton has pointed out,[13] some of the stated objectives scattered throughout the report seem plainly inconsistent, and that time and again the committee showed complete ignorance of basic work that had already been done in educational theory, as when they talk blandly of education according to needs, apparently having failed to appreciate that the concept of a need is intimately tied up with values, so that needs are not simple and neutral givens.[14] But I must stress again that it is not the ideas or proposals contained within the report that I am here concerned with. It is the nature of the discussion or reasoning that is employed to present the committee's views. What is primarily wrong with education at the moment is the widespread inability to improve the quality of thought about it. That is what the report exhibits and illustrates.

2.5 Some readers may feel that too much time has passed for it to be worth recalling Hall-Dennis. I have heard it said that the influence of the report on school practice in Ontario has waned and that "things have tightened up in the schools now." That argument misses the point that what is important about the report, why it is necessary to go on drawing attention to it, is its rhetoric rather than the views it puts forward. It also underplays the fact that in Ontario the impact of the report is still very much to be felt in three respects. Its rhetoric still imbues Ministry of Education directives and is still current amongst the establishment figures in the Ontario Teachers' Federation.[15] The practice that it hoped to inspire is still to be found extensively in the schools as the recent Hall-Carlton Study shows. Its rhetoric is still rampant in educational talk and writing.

i) *Ministry Directives*. In the past six years the requirements laid out in Ontario's Ministerial circulars have indeed been tightened up considerably and more specific demands have been made on the schools.[16] But even a quick glance at the 1977/8 Circular reveals that the whole Ontario programme of education is still based on ideas, typically espoused by the progressive tradition, that have not been adequately articulated or thought through. It is not necessarily false or improper to assert that education should be concerned "to help each student develop to the maximum his or her potential as an individual". But it is extremely obscure and therefore unhelpful and impractical.[17] For instance, just to scratch the surface of the conceptual problems here, what is one's 'potential as an individual'? I do not mean what, as a matter of fact, are you or I potentially capable of. I mean to ask, what do we mean by a person's potential? Is one born with an innate potential? Is one's potential created and developed by circumstance? If so, what factors help, what factors hinder the development of potential? Or is reference to someone's potential just a way of pointing out that what isn't apparent yet might become so? Is one's potential necessarily a good thing? Like it or not, we are here deeply embedded in extremely complicated questions about personal identity. In exactly the same way we may ask those who favour the terminology of 'realizing the self' whether they take the 'self' to be something innate or a product of circumstance.

What sense does it make, anyway, to talk of 'realizing' the self, if the self is essentially determined by one's environment? An acorn may, I suppose, be said to 'realize itself' in the oak tree. But the rock that has been shaped by centuries of wind and rain is not the 'realization of' the rather different substance that stood there millions of years ago. So, if (to simplify) we are doing what the Ministry tells us to do in order to ensure the 'self-realization' of the young, or to maximize their potential, it transpires that, for all anyone has so far said, we have no idea whether we *are* doing something appropriate to those ends, since we don't have much understanding of what they are. And partly for the same reason, partly because we just haven't thought about it enough, we have no obvious answer to the question "Why are you concentrating on realizing their selves or maximizing their potential?" Why not train them for a job that will be available? Why not do one of a dozen other things?

Realizing the self or individual development is the pivot on which the current Ministry directives turn, but there is much else in the directives and accompanying guidelines that echoes the report to which they are heir. "The school is to help each student develop . . . as a member of society who will think clearly, feel deeply and act wisely."[18] No doubt; but what counts as thinking clearly? Who is to say and on what grounds that the Marxist or the anarchist is not thinking clearly? What is a deep feeling? Is any deep feeling good? How do you recognize deep feelings? And surely no-one dare pretend that there are no problems about judging what constitutes a wise action.

What is really meant by phrases that trip so lightly off the tongue and sound so impressive to the ear as 'the dignity of work' or the statement that "the vital qualities of intellectual curiosity and imagination also require constant encouragement"?[19]

It may be said that when one is dealing with aims one has to be vague and that it is in the nature of aims that they should be vague. Indeed that claim is sometimes used as a reason for concentrating on behavioural objectives. But the claim is nonsense. Ultimate aims, because they are ultimate and distant, are very often broad and general; but it is imperative that they should not be vague, which is a quite different matter. ('Animal' is a broader term than 'dog', but it is not more vague. Lewis Carroll's 'Boojum' is no broader a term than 'dog', but it is extremely vague.) There is no such thing as a vague aim or a vague anything else in nature. There are only vague ideas about things in people's heads. The progressive rhetoric we are here considering is vague about aims. It is vague because it is ill thought out, and it is equally vague about immediate objectives. Thus we are told that compulsory credit courses in English studies are designed to "help students to develop effective communication skills" so that they are able "to learn how to organize ideas in a logical manner, and to communicate clearly and effectively with others."[20] But what precisely do these notions or concepts involve? What are effective communication skills? Can they be listed and lucidly explained, so that we know what we are trying to develop? What constitutes a logical manner? Who judges the effectiveness and clarity of others, and how?

Is this essay clearly written? If not, why not? What exactly is wrong with it? And what is involved in developing "an understanding of the Canadian identity . . . a reasoned pride in Canada . . . an understanding of fundamental concepts . . . justice, change, concern for others"?[21] Do you understand justice? I'm not sure that I even understand what it would be to understand justice.

I hope that enough has been said to show that Ontario Ministry of Education circulars and guidelines still contain much of the same rhetoric and the same kind of conceptual cloudiness that marked the Hall-Dennis report. Official educationalese is still pregnant with what Daly aptly characterized as molasses of this type: "In all learning situations, adolescents need sincerity, integrity, empathy and concern for those about them. Such an environment leaves individuals free to grow".[22] That *may* be true. But ugh! While we hide behind words in this way, words that placate all men and mean everything to all men and hence nothing in particular, we are making no real advance. Is there something lurking behind the appearance of all this rhetoric? It is a question of whether, putting aside the assumption that he must be, the Emperor is *actually* wearing any clothes.

ii) *School Practice*. Secondly, as has been the case with the Plowden report in Britain, the Hall-Dennis report has had far more and far more long-lasting practical effect in Ontario than one could possibly have foreseen, judging from the rapid and devastating critical reception it received. At the present time Ontario demands twenty-seven credits in all for high school students. The available courses are divided into four areas (communications, social studies, sciences, arts) and students must take at least three credits in each area. In addition the final twenty-seven credits must include two in English, two in mathematics, one in science, one in Canadian history and one in Canadian geography (or another in Canadian history). Superficially that may appear awesome and restrictive—a far cry from the *laissez-faire* approach of Hall-Dennis.[23] But in fact it remains the case, as many Ontario teachers will tell you, that the system is such as to allow the individual to spend most of his time doing practically anything. Thus, in one year a student might do three credits in drafting, three in floriculture, three in horticulture and three in merchandising. Furthermore, what actually goes on in those courses, or any others, including the compulsory credits, may vary a great deal from school to school and class to class, in view of the latitude of interpretation possible with the Ministry guidelines. I am not trying to demean such excellent pursuits as horticulture, but it's a little difficult to see the immediate connection between a schooling of this type and the professed aim of enabling students to think clearly, feel deeply and act wisely.

More generally, the impact of Hall-Dennis on the schools may be gauged from the Hall-Carlton study. Entitled *Basic Skills at School and Work*, this is a comprehensive attitudinal study of an Ontario township fictitiously called Albertown carried out by Oswald Hall and Richard Carlton. It contains a lot of interesting information about the educational views of various segments of the population. For example, it transpires that within the teaching profession everyone is inclined to put the blame for perceived problems on the stage prior to that with which he is concerned, until finally all the blame falls on the elementary sector; that difference and variety disconcert children and yet remain features of today's schools; that most employers are interested only in crude questions of reliability and skills; that many students feel they have been deprived of something in that they have not received a good grounding in basics (even if, according to the testimony of their teachers, many were bored when the teacher tried to deal with such matters). All of these findings are important and are pertinent to the wider interests of this essay. But for the moment the point to stress is that the study clearly shows widespread dissatisfaction and disappointment, amongst both teachers and students, which is seen as the product of a loosening up of and within the schooling system, which in itself is seen as a consequence of the Hall-Dennis report. Of course, this is not to say that the perceptions of these people necessarily have any objective validity; still less is it to say that here is evidence that the schools have failed. (On some criteria they have apparently succeeded.) But if the testimony of this township can be relied upon and generalized from within the context of Ontario, it shows that progressive rhetoric had considerable impact on practice.

iii) *Educational Discourse*. Finally, and in my view most significantly, the style of rhetoric, as opposed to the content, espoused by the progressive tradition is still rampant in educational discourse. This is nowhere more apparent than in what is characteristically known as the back-lash to progressivism itself. In Britain the polarization technique was blatantly adopted by those who got together to contribute to what they named the *Black Papers* in education in which appeared such emotive titles as "The Sleep of Reason" and "Is it too late?"[24] More generally we see the same polarization when progressivism is portrayed as a monolithic system and dismissed as 'the wrong way'; we see the same technique of thinking in slogans with cries such as 'back to basics', the same love of would-be panaceas in the suggestion that we should 'tighten up on discipline', and the same gross oversimplification in the claim that 'standards have dropped'.

2.6 I have tried to suggest that the progressive tradition, exemplified in Ontario by the Hall-Dennis report, has had some impact. There is also some evidence that currently a mood of disillusionment with progressive-inspired practice has set in amongst teachers and even students. This, I must confess, seems all to the good to me, if it results in a rejection of basic axioms implicit in progressive ideology, such as that having a kind heart is as good as having a coherent plan of action in education or that the only real questions are methodological, so that aims can remain on the level of woolly and cosy platitudes. However, we must not fail to appreciate that the worst thing about this tradition has been its style and that we must ensure that we do not retain it. We should not necessarily be looking for simple, precise and measurable educational goals and strategies as a reaction to the woolliness of progressivism. We must look first for the clearly articulated and the well-reasoned. For the truth is that education may not be a simple and quantifiable endeavour either as a whole or in its various parts. It may be complex and ideal in its nature, in which case to simplify and to reduce to the attainable is to distort. What we need to do most of all is think things through. That is what the progressive tradition inadvertently teaches us.

Notes

1. For a more detailed analysis of the radical tradition, see Robin Barrow, *Radical Education*, London: Martin Robertson and Co. Ltd., 1978.
2. A. S. Neill, for example, remarks, "my primary job is not the reformation of society, but the bringing of happiness to some few children." *Summerhill, A Radical Approach to Child Rearing*, New York: Hart Publishing Co., 1960, p. 23.
3. *Radical Education*, op. cit., chs. 2 and 3.
4. See R. F. Dearden, *The Philosophy of Primary Education*, London: Routledge and Kegan Paul, 1968, ch. 3, for a basic analytic look at the concept of growth.
5. See Robin Barrow, *Moral Philosophy for Education*, London: George Allen and Unwin Ltd., 1975, chs. 4 and 12, for a discussion of A. S. Neill on freedom. See also *Radical Education*, op. cit., ch. 4.
6. E. M. Hall and L. A. Dennis, *Living and Learning*, Toronto: Ontario Department of Education, 1968.
7. *Basic Skills at School and Work*, op. cit.
8. *Children and their Primary Schools*, A Report of the Central Advisory Council for Education (England), London: H.M.S.O., Volume I, 1967.
9. The evidence for this assertion is to be found in *Basic Skills at School and Work*, op. cit.
10. James Daly, *Education or Molasses? A Critical Look at the Hall-Dennis Report*, Ancaster: Cromlech Press, 1969. B. Crittenden (ed.), *Means and Ends in Education, Comments on Living and Learning*, Toronto: O.I.S.E., Occasional Papers 2, 1969.
11. W. G. Davis in *Re-Thinking Education*, Toronto: O.I.S.E., 1969, p. 8.
12. Ontario Teachers' Federation *Living and Learning*, Toronto: Ontario Teachers' Federation, abridged edition, 1968, p. 26.

13. James M. Paton in *Re-Thinking Education*, op. cit., p. 43 ff.
14. See also R. F. Dearden, "'Needs' in education", in R. F. Dearden, P. H. Hirst, R. S. Peters (eds.), *Education and the Development of Reason*, London: Routledge and Kegan Paul, 1972, p. 50.
15. In private conversation with me, an Executive Officer of the Ontario Teachers' Federation asserted that many of the Hall-Dennis committee were his nominees. He showed no awareness at all of the shortcomings of the report and was evidently unfamiliar with most of the standard criticism.
16. Known as circular H.S.I. forms, the first appeared in 1972-73, clearly influenced by the Hall-Dennis Report.
17. The quotation is taken from the section of Circular H.S.I. entitled, "Philosophical objectives", Toronto: Ontario Ministry of Education, 1977-78, p. 1. It is perhaps worth commenting on that barbarism. The objectives in question are not philosophical but educational (or should be). There seems to be a confusion between the correct observation that there are many vital philosophical questions to be raised about aims and objectives, and the meaningless assertion that aims and objectives *are* philosophical (with the strange implication that only philosophers need have them or bother about them).
18. Ibid., p. 1.
19. Ibid., p. 1.
20. English Curriculum Guideline, Senior Division, Toronto: Ontario Ministry of Education, 1977, p. 4.
21. History Curriculum Guideline, Intermediate Division, Toronto: Ontario Ministry of Education, 1977, p. 6.
22. Ibid., p. 4.
23. Although the four areas interestingly resemble the three proposed by Hall-Dennis—Communications, Environmental Studies and the Humanities, p. 180.
24. C. B. Cox and A. E. Dyson (eds.), *Black Papers One, Two and Three*, London: The Critical Quarterly Society, n.d.

CHAPTER 3

The Radical Challenge[1]

3.1 The tendency of the progressive tradition to assume that all that matters is to have one's heart in the right place and that all educational problems are essentially problems of attitude and methodology has resulted in its failure to produce a coherent and communicable educational theory. By contrast the radical tradition has made some noteworthy criticisms of schooling and produced some important insights. This is largely because it has tried to face up to the basic conceptual questions (for example, the distinction between 'education' and 'schooling') and has recognized the need to go right back to the beginning and ask what we are trying to achieve and why. As mentioned above, it has also appreciated the importance of looking at schooling and education in a social context. This is particularly clear in the work of Jean Jacques Rousseau who may, with some justice, be seen as the father of many contemporary radical themes. Rousseau makes the political-educational link very clear both by dint of writing the *Social Contract* and *Emile* as complementary works and by saying (notwithstanding frequent and misleading quotations of the term 'noble savage') that Emile is not "a savage" to be sent "back to the woods."[2] Having been brought up in isolation, he is ultimately supposed to go back into society as it is and, as a result of his particular education, to cope with it without being gulled by its falsity and conceit. If all people were brought up in the manner of Emile, then, according to Rousseau, we would have the appropriate conditions in which the General Will might function, which in turn would mean that we could expect a perfect democratic state, firmly based on a social contract between citizens.[3]

3.2 It is important to appreciate at the outset that Rousseau does *not* offer the *laissez-faire*, permissive approach to education that some progressives have claimed he does. He is the manipulator of all time—the Machiavelli of education. His position could be said to be encapsulated in a proper understanding of his claim that "the child" should "do nothing because he is told; nothing is good for him but what he recognises as good."[4] Rousseau does not mean, as is sometimes assumed, that we should let the child do what he wants or act just as the spirit moves him. He means that it is our job as teachers to bring the child to understand why he should do things and to enable him to see the point of doing this rather than that, and that we should not be content merely to issue commands. The fact remains that according to Rousseau it is *we* who must decide what should go on; *we* are in charge, not Emile. We should be concerned, Rousseau continues, "with what we can do for our pupil through our choice of the circumstances in which he shall be placed."[5] In other words we organize the stimuli, the opportunities, and the direction of his upbringing. By the end of Emile's schooling, as Rousseau freely and frankly admits, all that we "have gained has been won by force or guile; . . . " Emile's obedience was gained by constraint and deceit.[6] To Rousseau, in the last analysis, the science of pedagogy is the art of timing: what matters is to be ready at the optimum moment to take advantage of Emile's curiosity or interest. But there is no suggestion that we should be *governed* or *limited* by that.

It is necessary to have a proper understanding of Rousseau's view that "that man is truly free who desires what he is able to perform, and does what he desires."[7] This amounts to equating freedom with the sense of freedom. It is also important to recognize that his view of happiness is very similar and is likewise bound up with the idea of being satisfied with one's circumstances.[8] Rousseau's concern with freedom and happiness therefore lacks that element of cosy and bland idealism which marks the interest of the progressives in those concepts. To some extent he is proposing a very realistic objective: that of bringing people up to recognize and to be satisfied with various straightforward everyday restraints, so that they are not irked by them.

Upbringing as it is, Rousseau feels, restrains people unnecessarily and unnaturally. It is that which he objects to rather than restraint itself and it is that which leads him to say that current educational practice does not involve true education. Hence he is led to make the distinction between schooling and education which has proved so fruitful in the radical tradition. The upbringing of his time he castigates as a mere schooling: a conditioning into the passive acceptance of the prejudices and whims of the time—into much foolishness and nonsense. What is wrong with it is that it is nonsense, not that it might be characterized as conditioning, habituation or socialization. True education might likewise socialize—but it would socialize people to what Rousseau regards as true and worthwhile.

3.3 The radical tradition also owes to Rousseau the first formulation of a number of important observations and perceptions which need to be considered in their own right.

a) First, there is recognition of the phenomenon now generally termed the *hidden curriculum*. By hidden curriculum is meant such content as is taught but is not overtly timetabled by the school. An obvious example of the hidden curriculum in most schools would be the values and attitudes that are promoted steadily, sometimes overtly, sometimes covertly, throughout the school day. Rousseau, interestingly, shows acute awareness of this phenomenon in relation to the sphere of medicine. Here he anticipates much of Ivan Illich's recent work when he suggests that we learn a great deal from the medical profession that is not overtly stated, such as, that only doctors can cure and that only certain states count as sickness, which they are being defined by the profession.[9]
b) An extension of the hidden curriculum phenomenon is the issue of institutional dominance which is most obviously drawn attention to by Illich and Reimer, but also touched upon by Postman and Weingartner when they stress the McLuhan thesis that the medium is the message. The essence of this point is the claim that the

way in which we present knowledge modifies its nature, and that institutions in particular deaden, alter and sometimes even falsify it. Illich and Reimer believe that the institution of schooling as such inevitably and automatically distorts the educational content and causes untold damage. For example, as a result of institutionalization, we come to believe that schools are the proper and only channel for true learning; we consequently devalue what we might learn at home, pick up on the job or read in some book that is not presented as an academic and scholarly volume. Again, it is alleged, schools make us confuse ritual and substance: we admire the Ph.D. rather than the argument put forward by a given individual. Furthermore, schools, according to Illich, "create certainties . . . [which] deaden the heart."[10]

c) Thirdly, the radical tradition deplores the all-pervasive way in which education is hamstrung by the grade system and the paraphernalia of assessment. As Ian Lister has observed "The social power of the educational system lies in its power to print its own money",[11] which is to say the reason why the school system has such power is that it gives the individual the qualifications that serve as a passport to advancement in our society. One cannot deny, I think, even prior to critical reflection on the matter, that the attainment of good grades is in itself a poor sort of educational objective; that a centralized examination system must tend to foster irrelevance; that the perceived value of work in respect of grading must tend to affect people's general evaluation of the work in question; and that qualifications tend to determine the status we accord to individuals. The whole system of assessment is in danger of getting out of hand and is far from perfect even on its own terms.

d) Fourthly, there is evidently something in the radical contention that knowledge is not an unqualified given and that things are, at any rate in some respects and in some sense, as you see them. Certainly we do, up to a point, "'make' the reality we perceive rather than passively 'receive' or 'reflect' it," to quote Postman and

Weingartner.[12] When rain falls from the sky, as they say, some head for shelter and others continue walking. And we must surely grant that "their perceptions of 'what is happening' are different as reflected in the fact that they 'do' different things. The fact that both groups will agree to the sentence 'It is raining' does not mean that they perceive the 'event' in the same way."[13] More will need to be said on this, as on the other points here listed, in a moment. But for the moment we may say: yes, that is so.

e) Fifthly, Postman and Weingartner give prominence to the vivid term 'crap-detecting' and argue that what true education involves is more of the spirit of the crap-detector to blow away what Rousseau had scornfully characterized as the received opinion of those with influence and power. It is difficult not to endorse the broad demand of the radicals for critical thought; but there are certain problems in the conception, to be noticed below.

f) Sixthly, it has always been maintained in the radical tradition, again in the words of Postman and Weingartner, that "it is also . . . insane . . . for a teacher to 'teach' something unless his students require it for some identifiable and important purpose, which is to say, for some purpose that is related to the life of the learner."[14] That as stated may seem unexceptionable; but it too will need further elucidation and comment.

3.4 These perceptions, if taken seriously, suggest that we need to take a good hard look at what we do with that vast number of students whom we drag up through grades to about their twenty-fifth year. The observations, if they turn out to carry any weight, would certainly combine to establish the point that schooling is by no means one and the same thing as education: indeed, in important respects the two may be pulling in opposite directions. It would seem that standard school practice might amount to little more than gentling the populace by feeding them the current follies of our age.

But if we now subject these ideas to a brief critical examination it will become clear that despite the percipience of their criticisms of the current situation, the radicals have not always fully understood the limits and implications of their own points and have thus come to propound positive proposals that constitute no real solution.

a) As to the hidden curriculum, it is important to recognize that it *is* there. Illich claims that part of its content is the lesson that "valuable learning is the result of attendance"[15] and, conversely, that only peripheral and non-serious learning can come about outside school. Reimer cites what he regards as distorted conceptions of freedom, equality, progress and research and the view that competition is necessary and desirable as elements of the hidden curriculum.

However, although the claim that there is a hidden curriculum can hardly be gainsaid, the assumption that it could be got rid of seems badly misplaced and the assumption that it should be, if it could be, highly questionable. It might well be argued that the hidden curriculum is not something that has been unearthed by the radicals, so much as a deliberate and important longstanding aspect of schooling. The English Public Schools (i.e., private schools), for example, have always prided themselves on their character-building tendencies as much as on anything else, and yet the Public School spirit is essentially the product of the non-timetabled ethos of the place—the hidden curriculum, in fact. The truth is that the so-called hidden curriculum is an essential and inevitable part of schooling. In its widest sense the term is practically synonymous with 'influence'; and influence cannot be avoided, certainly not by deschooling which would merely remove one source of influence on children while leaving a hundred others such as the example of parents and of peer groups, advertising, television and so on. But what we can reasonably say is that we do need to be alert to the phenomenon of the hidden curriculum and that it may need to be controlled. Certainly our students should at some point be brought to an awareness of the phenomenon.

In short there is a hidden curriculum and to some extent no doubt it does foster the values cited by the radicals. As against that it may be argued that some at least are values that we want fostered and that some kind of non-overt formation of values and attitudes is inevitable. But what is true is that *bona fide* curriculum reforms must also involve reform of the hidden curriculum.

b) The deschoolers propose as a solution dis-establishing the schools. It is probably true that the institution of schooling has evolved a logic and momentum of its own—and it is arguable that that logic is pretty poor. There is not much doubt that the system of schooling is itself shaping the next generation, as it did us, and in some respects shaping it none too surely. But, as I have already observed in reference to the more specific question of the hidden curriculum, to do away with schooling is to do away with one set of influences only; it would not do away with influence itself and would therefore not solve the alleged problem. Schools are not the only institutions with which we are plagued and doing away with schooling would therefore not amount to de-institutionalizing the mentality of the next generation. Even if it were possible to do away with the monolithic giant school system, we would still face the problem of non-rational, externally imposed suggestions being brought to bear on people. One important positive point about an organized system of schooling is that it at least carries within it the potential to promote the antidote to the force of the hidden curriculum and institutionalization systematically—namely critical inquiry into oneself and one's surroundings. And that is surely what should be done rather than indulging in the idle speculation that non-rational influence could somehow be avoided altogether.

c) In briefly considering the question of grading, I should like to distinguish between the practice of assessing student progress in some way or another, the practice of using a public system of grades to advertise the assessment made, the practice of awarding certificates, diplomas and degrees as public stamps of approval, and various specific forms of examination. There is no doubt in my mind that the radicals are correct in saying that most of this area has got out of hand so that diplomas are demanded for everything, the value of certificates and degrees is minimal as a result of inflationary awards, people are assessed by their paper qualifications, and work programmes are dominated by the examination system. If schools are going to get back into the job of providing education, which unlike the deschoolers I think they can, they are going to have to liberate themselves from the tyranny of the system to some extent. Nonetheless education *is* about standards amongst other things. It is not necessarily about objective or public standards (though sometimes it may be that too) but it is certainly concerned with individual progress—and progress implies some measurable advance, which in turn means that there must be some form of assessment wherever we are trying to educate people.

d) Turning now to the fourth observation of the radicals, that the medium is the message and things are as you see them, the sad truth is that the most sensible of Postman and Weingartner's remarks upon the subject have already been quoted. I do not intend to examine here the quasi-nonsensical remarks made by some of the contributors to a recent volume entitled *Knowledge and Control* to the effect that all reality is how you see it—which doesn't even make a logically tenable thesis, since, if it were so, it would have to apply to the thesis (which is presumably being expounded as some kind of real and significant truth) itself.[16] I shall stop short of examining the view that "all knowledge is socially constructed" or the assertion that "rationality itself is an arbitrary convention." But the reader should be warned that such confused and extreme lunacies do hover on the fringe of the radical tradition.

Postman and Weingartner's more extreme statements on the subject include the following: "reality is a perception located somewhere behind the eyes"; "we 'make' the reality we perceive"; "whatever is out there isn't anything until we make it something and then it 'is' whatever we make it"; and it is not for us (as teachers) to exclude anything as not "germane" to a discussion.[17] It must be admitted that most of these could be shrugged off and excused as mere enthusiastic overstatements, since most of the thesis they imply is subsequently contradicted by Postman and Weingartner themselves.[18] But it is important to get this matter clear. Reality is by definition what is outside our minds: what we mean by reality is that which is the case regardless of idiosyncratic opinions, subjective opinions or personal point of view. Furthermore, although, of course, there are profound philosophical questions about whether anything is real, whether we exist or are fragments of a dream, and so forth, it is insane to deny that there is any reality in an everyday sense; and it is absurd to teach as if there were not. Whatever we do, we must maintain the distinction between such things as the table before me and the observation that two and two equal four on the one hand (to cite two very different types of reality), and the pink elephant in the corner on the other. Provided we cling steadfastly to that distinction, then we can afford to and should take due note of the sensible part of the radical message which is the point that we do interpret as we observe. Few things if any are simply given in an unambiguous manner. Furthermore, it may be conceded that all claims to knowledge should strictly speaking remain provisional claims. But it is any given claim that is provisional and not knowledge itself. It is simply a mistake to confuse the truth that we may always be mistaken with the absurdity that there is nothing to be mistaken about, which is the implication of extreme subjectivism. This matter may be put in perspective by reference to the 'rain' example, given above. From the observation that different people do different things, and thus may be said to have different perceptions of reality, it does not follow that it was not as a matter of fact raining. It is not only our perceptions that limit us: there are facts as well and they set the limits within which we may safely—or, as we sometimes say, sanely

—manoeuvre. And consequently one thing the teacher must do, in the interests of reality, truth, knowledge and sanity is to arbitrate. As Postman and Weingartner themselves finally sheepishly admit in a transparent *volte-face*: "We still need to know if someone's statements about the world are 'better' than someone else's."[19]

e) If Postman and Weingartner seem a little confused on the issue of knowledge and reality, they are at any rate on to something important with their notion of crap-detecting. We cannot afford, and those of us who favour autonomy and democracy cannot approve, an education system that throws up docile individuals dominated by received opinion and accepted perceptions (the stress, of course, must fall on 'dominated'; there is nothing necessarily wrong with sharing current opinions). But once again, and this is characteristic of the radical tradition which is often careless in its excitement, Postman and Weingartner do not give us much help in coming to a more precise understanding of what is involved in being a crap-detector. It is not clear, for example, how we should distinguish between the crap-detector, who is not dominated by current prejudice, and the crapper, who spews indiscriminately on the accepted. Most of the terms that are thrown in to elucidate this concept are precisely those that exercise the wit of serious educational thinkers. For instance, Postman and Weingartner seek to explain the concept in terms of being a good learner, confidence, being aware of what is relevant to one's survival, self-reliance, flexibility and inventiveness. But that explanation doesn't make it any easier to see what we need to do to develop good crap-detectors. To be told that we must produce 'flexible', 'inventive' and 'creative' minds is not in itself much use. What is a 'creative' mind? How does one produce the 'inventive' and 'flexible' mind? This not the place to pursue those questions so much as to draw attention to the need to do so. But I will venture to doubt if it is warranted or helpful to refer to such things as creativity and flexibility as if they were straightforward faculties. I suspect that most of these mental concepts are best seen as a mixture of character traits, a certain disposition and a range of competences that may vary in their transferability.

Postman and Weingartner are anxious to promote the inquiry method of teaching. But they fail to make an important distinction between the conditions under which something may take place and the conditions likely to promote the development of that same thing. What they illustrate well is the inquiry method in action with reasonably mature students.[20] It is not clear that they have produced any evidence to support the contention that a diet of inquiry method from kindergarten onwards is sufficient to promote the crap-detecting mentality. The obvious objection to too much stress on inquiry is that at some point there must be a base on which to build: inquiry can only be pursued from a secure basis. You have to know something, or at any rate assume that you do, in order to get a critical foothold from which to challenge other assumed givens. There is also a tendency for the radicals to talk as if education is primarily concerned with new knowledge. But the conditions under which real advances in knowledge are made may very well differ from the optimum conditions under which current knowledge is assimilated. Yet it is surely the latter which is the main concern of the schools. And when it comes to the stock of current knowledge that we may wish to disseminate, it is surely immediately obvious that no one technique will always be the most efficacious: it is probably best to learn to ride a bike by doing it, but it is doubtful whether such an approach even makes sense in respect of, say, learning physics, since what doing physics consists in is not exclusively revealed in observable behaviour, but is crucially bound up with why and how the physicist does what he does.

Postman and Weingartner claim that "Knowledge is produced in response to questions. And new knowledge results from the asking of new questions about old questions."[21] That is possibly an accurate observation about how people generally come to acquire knowledge in the first place; but it should not be confused with a statement about the nature of knowledge. The truth is that, to increase one's personal store of knowledge, it is by no means always most efficacious to inquire after it single-handed, even if the inquiry method deserves a place in education. As so often, the radicals overstate their case.

f) That education should concern itself with what is useful is one of those vacuous contentions that run about in educational literature for years because nobody has the heart to kill such obvious truths. True, yes, but, to measure it by its own yardstick, useless. For who is to determine what is useful? Useful in respect of what? Are we talking about what is as a matter of fact useful in some specifiable respect, what appears to be useful, or what turns out to have been useful after the event? The extraordinary thing about the radical conception of the useful is that it is construed only in terms of whatever is seen as immediately necessary to basic economic survival. Thus, in Goodman the demand for useful schooling is equated with the demand that students should do things like apprentice themselves to a paying trade. In Neill, subjects like Latin are dismissed on the grounds that they have no crude utility. No doubt the radicals are right to draw attention to economic utility as one important factor. The schools should give some thought to how students are going to have to earn their living and survive in society—more than they have in the past, perhaps. But it is equally important to stress both that there are alternative ways of interpreting 'useful' and that it is the long term that needs to be considered. To make the point crudely: at the present time it might be most useful for young Jim to be trained as a telephone operator; but in the long run, even in crude economic terms, preoccupation with schooling of that sort could be disastrous for all. In any case we must avoid being exclusively wed to a crude economic interpretation of what is useful. The useful can only be determined in the light of our aims and objectives and it is here that we need to recall (as the radicals seldom do despite the fact that in essence they share it) the ideal of a thriving democratic community of autonomous individuals. To the effective and satisfactory realization of that ideal a number of character traits and intellectual skills, some of which have traditionally been seen as schooling objectives, retain their usefulness to a far greater extent than some of the more obvious and mechanical skills that some enjoin us to promote and develop.

3.5 Usefulness is one of the key concepts with which the radicals operate. Others, each of which requires a brief comment, are nature, reality and learning.

a) The word 'natural' may mean many things; for example, spontaneous, innate, typical. In one sense it is used as a normative term, practically synonymous with 'right and proper.' The unfortunate consequence of there being a normative sense of the term is that the connotations of desirability are carried over quite undeservedly to other senses. Thus, people tend to assume uncritically that whatever is 'natural', in any sense of the word, must be good, which is, of course, simply untrue. But study of the radical tradition reveals something much more serious than its unconscious play with the word 'nature.' What emerges is that the radicals believe unquestioningly, and sometimes perhaps unconsciously, in a fixed human nature or, as it might be better to phrase it, in innate human characteristics, both mental and moral. That is to say, most of the radicals I have referred to believe that people are born with a more or less determinate level of goodness or badness and wisdom or folly. When I say that they believe in innate human nature in this sense, I do not mean that they openly avow it. I mean that they make claims and build up a thesis that only makes sense on this assumption. Thus, Neill talks of Freddy Beethoven and Charlie Einstein emerging in later life no matter what happens to them at school, and he distinguishes between people "who have the innate ability and [the] wish to be scholars" and those who are born "only fit to sweep the street."[22] Goodman explicitly endorses the view that only about fifteen per cent of students ever could be capable of learning well "by books and study in an academic setting."[23] Besides, the entire radical thesis that current schooling distorts true human nature only makes sense if there is something in individual natures other than the patterns that can be imposed by circumstance and the changes brought about by the environment.

The objections to this assumption of innate human nature are these:

1) First, in the form implied by most of their writing, the belief that there is an innate nature in the new-born individual is certainly false. That is to say there is absolutely no reason to accept the view that people are born with a fixed moral character, determinate intellectual ability and a delimited range of interest.
2) Secondly, the view may very well be false in any significant sense. That is to say the extent to which we are the product of genetic endowment, whether hereditary or otherwise, may in most cases be far less significant than the extent to which we can be shaped by our environment.
3) Thirdly, and crucially, this view makes a nonsense of the whole burden of their fear about various forms of influence on the individual (such as the hidden curriculum) and their egalitarian assumptions about the consequences of deschooling.

Their problem is this: either the whole apparatus of character formation is to be condemned on the grounds that it is an assault on the true nature of the individual (in which case we must incidentally face up to a world in which people are inescapably different in ability, talent, interest and so on). Or we can achieve egalitarian goals, in which case there are not significant innate differences, and it cannot be legitimate to castigate the present school system for assaulting and distorting human nature.

b) The notion of reality is very much to the fore in the radical tradition. Rousseau, Goodman, Postman and others all object to a great deal of current practice on the grounds that it is unreal. However the 'real' tends to be construed very broadly so that it is sometimes contrasted with convention, sometimes with opinion, with appearance, with falsehood and so on. Furthermore, it is instructive to note how, while using the same word, different radicals interpret reality in quite different ways. Rousseau characterizes reality more or less entirely in terms of the negativization of social or civilized habits: man's life would be real, if he would rid himself of social norms. Goodman, on the other hand, defines reality in terms of current practice or what is the case, so that his plea for more concern for reality is a plea for facing up to the way the world is.[24] Postman and Weingartner, as is already evident, define reality in terms of how things appear to the individual. It should at once be clear that, potentially interesting as the concept of reality is, in the radical tradition the word serves mainly as a contemporary variant of 'natural' and is subject to the same criticism as pertains to the radical use of 'natural' and 'useful'. The term has considerable emotive force but very little in the way of clear and consistent descriptive meaning.

c) When it comes to 'learning,' the radicals make some of their most implausible claims, largely because they confuse conceptual and empirical questions. That is to say they fail to distinguish questions about what 'learning' is or what it means, and questions about how and where it may take place. If we take 'learning' to mean something like the acquisition of new knowledge in such a way as to be able to make effective use of it, then it is at once apparent that a wild claim such as Goodman's that "Nothing can be . . . learned at all . . . unless it meets, need, desire, curiosity or fantasy"[25] is simply false.

It is absolutely certain, as most of us can testify from personal experience, that one can learn things which one is not interested in learning, indeed that one can learn things in which one never develops an interest. This is not to recommend that we try to teach without interesting students; it is merely to observe that it can be done.

Once the extravagances of the radical claims about learning are ironed out, we are in a position to resist their uneconomic and unsystematic demand for leaving the question of what is to be learned to the spontaneous enthusiasm of the individual. We can then replace that with the following rather more sane approach: consider rationally what things are most worth learning or most useful in the light of our chosen ideal, and seek to promote interest in them and indeed in learning and the acquisition of knowledge for their own sakes. It is, of course, a consequence of their belief in innate human nature, that the radicals do not think in terms of creating interest. But that is surely one of the most important tasks of the teacher.

3.6 And so we come to the conclusion of all this for the contemporary radicals.[26] What they propose that we should do would amount to leaving the upbringing or education of our children to chance. That, needless to say, is not what they think they are proposing to do; but it is what their proposals would lead to. They repeatedly appeal to the educational environment, which is to say, ideally, society, and they expect people to be educated by mere existence in that environment. But here, clearly, we have a classic instance of the chicken and the egg problem. Obviously, if we lived in a society which was educative, we should not need to take any further steps to educate. But equally clearly we do not live in such a society, as the radicals have most eloquently told us. The question therefore is what happens now, at this point in time, if we disestablish the school, or disband any clear curriculum? And the answer is that we will end up with a number of very different individuals in terms of character, interest and ability, not because they were born different (as the radicals slyly imply) but because they are born into different environments in this far from equal or uniform society.

What it may be asked is wrong with that? To a certain type of nineteenth century liberal very little. But the radicals do not see themselves as *laissez-faire* liberals. The objection to this for them ought to be that it does nothing to achieve their political ideals. (It would be unwise to assert that this approach *could* not result in a utopia such as they envisage; but there is certainly no obvious reason to suppose that it *would*.) What the radicals do is throw away the great opportunity that schooling gives us to *give* children talents and interests, to *bring* people together, to *forge* the ideal community. Because of their confused belief in innate human nature and learning as exclusively a product of interest, because of their naive view of how to calculate what is useful, they overstress the importance of their many perceptive criticisms of the school system and propose to do without it. Whereas the obvious and indeed only practical solution is to *use* the school system to develop in people an awareness of its deficiencies.

Far from relaxing the grip of the school, we need in some respects to increase it to meet the very shortcomings noted by the radicals.

3.7 Finally it should be noted that although I have concentrated largely on American authors in this chapter, Canada has its own share of radical educationalists who expound very similar theses. John Bremer, the author of *A matrix for modern education*, and recently Commissioner of Education in British Columbia, is one prominent example. Others will be found contributing to such volumes as *The politics of the Canadian Public School* and *Options: reforms and alternatives for Canadian education*.[27]

Notes

1. See below 3.7 and note 27.
2. Jean Jacques Rousseau, *Emile*, Barbara Foxley (transl.), London: J. M. Dent and Sons Ltd., Everyman edition, n.d., p. 217.
3. For a more detailed examination of Rousseau's political views and how they combine with his educational views, see *Radical Education*, op. cit., chs. 2 and 3.
4. Emile, op. cit., p. 141.
5. Ibid., p. 181.
6. Ibid., p. 281.
7. Ibid., p. 48.
8. "True happiness consists in decreasing the difference between

our desires and our powers, in establishing a perfect equilibrium between the power and the will." *Emile*, op. cit., p. 44.

9. *Emile*, op. cit., p. 22 ff. Cf. I. Illich, *Medical Nemesis*, London: Calder and Boyars, 1975.
10. I. Illich, *Celebration of Awareness*, Garden City, New York: Doubleday and Co. Inc., 1970, p. 11.
11. Ian Lister, "Should schools survive?" in Ian Lister (ed.), *Deschooling*, London: Cambridge University Press, 1974, p. 88.
12. N. Postman and C. Weingartner, *Teaching as a Subversive Activity*, New York: Dell Publishing Co., A Delta Book, 1969, p. 86.
13. Ibid., p. 91.
14. Ibid., p. 42.
15. I. Illich, "Schooling: the ritual of progress' in Ian Lister (ed.), *Deschooling*, op. cit., p. 65.
16. Michael F. Young (ed.), *Knowledge and Control, New Directions for the Sociology of Education*, London: Collier-Macmillan, 1971.
17. *Teaching as a Subversive Activity*, op. cit., pp. 91, 86, 99 and 36.
18. See my *Radical Education*, op. cit., ch. 7.
19. *Teaching as a Subversive Activity*, op. cit., p. 104.
20. Ibid., ch. 5.
21. Ibid., p. 23.
22. *Summerhill*, op. cit., p. 4.
23. Paul Goodman, "Freedom and Learning: the need for choice" in R. Hooper (ed.), *The Curriculum: Context, Design and Development*, Edinburgh: Oliver and Boyd, 1971, p. 109. Compare Goodman, *Compulsory Miseducation*, New York: Vintage Books, Random House Inc., 1964, p. 113.
24. "Freedom and Learning: the need for choice" in *The Curriculum: Context, Design and Development*, op. cit., p. 107.
25. Ibid., p. 107.
26. What follows does not apply to Rousseau whose overall approach would succeed in remoulding Emile in the shape that he, Rousseau, desires.
27. See John Bremer, *A matrix for modern education*, Toronto: McClelland and Stewart Ltd., 1975; George Martell (ed.), *The politics of the Canadian public school*, Toronto: James Lewis and Samuel, 1974; Terence Morrison and Anthony Burton (eds.), *Options: reforms and alternatives for Canadian education*, Toronto: Holt, Rinehart and Winston, 1973. See also Niall Byrne and Jack Quarter (eds.), *Must schools fail? The growing debate in Canadian Education*, Toronto: McClelland and Stewart Ltd., 1972 and the *May 1st Manual for a school day which serves the working class*, prepared by the militants of the C.E.Q. (Centrale de l'Enseignement du Québec), April, 1975.

CHAPTER 4

The School Curriculum

4.1 One thing the radicals are right about is that education and politics are linked. However convincing it may be to analyze the concept of education exclusively in terms of knowledge for its own sake, the fact is that the educational system is concerned with more than knowledge for its own sake. It plays a decisive part in the upbringing of children and that involves more than the traditionalist conception of education. It is silly to imagine that it was just conceptual confusion that caused a local Ontario paper recently to fulminate against the wastefulness of our expensive education on the grounds that it has failed to produce various specific kinds of skilled persons which, apparently, the economy and society as a whole need or want. Regardless of any particular conceptions of education, the local paper thinks the school system of a country ought to do something about job preparation. Similarly many people think that schools ought to do something about social problems such as rape, or raise the consciousness of people who are not aware that they are unconscious. There may be good arguments against such views, but they cannot convincingly be dismissed solely on the grounds that it is a matter of conceptual truth that education is not about things like strategies for avoiding rape, pursuing doctrinaire objectives or providing vocational skills. For, in reply, the schools may quite reasonably claim that they should do more than educate. Indeed, if the deschoolers are right in saying that the schools try to do too many different kinds of things, and must consequently fail to do any of them well, a quite reasonable response might be *not* to deschool, but merely to kick education out of the schools. I think therefore that it is a mistake for us to confine our interest to education; our interest should surely be in the whole question of upbringing, and that means that anything we say will, ultimately, presuppose some kind of socio-political aim or objective.

4.2 As explained above (1.10), I am assuming that we are concerned to produce a thriving community of autonomous and democratic citizens.

By 'autonomous' I understand one who thinks rationally for himself, one who is concerned that there should be good reason for what is done, and one who, though he may see good reason to abide by particular authorities at particular times, does not see the fact of somebody being in authority as in itself a good reason for doing what he says. (Being an authority on something is distinct from being in authority and can constitute a good reason for commanding respect or obedience.) There are two points to be noted about this account: first, 'autonomy' is a dispositional and a degree word. One does not have to exercise autonomy all the time in respect of everything to merit the label 'autonomous.' Secondly, rational thinking is built into the concept. It is not sufficient that a person tries to act on his own reasoning, according to my conception; that reasoning must be rational in the sense of non-fallacious and appropriate, though this too is a matter of degree. Furthermore, an autonomous man might be evil, selfish, a recluse or heaven knows what else, which is why it is important to include the word 'democratic'. What I mean by a 'democratic' individual is one who is committed to certain values and equipped with certain attitudes.[1] To be specific: the 'democratic' man is one who believes in the value of equal happiness for all and such material equality as that may necessitate, the value of freedom up to the point where it militates against the well-being of others, the value of absolute freedom of expression, the value of impartiality, and the value of such procedural devices as may best serve those other values; as to attitudes, he is tolerant of diversity, fond of his freedom, responsible with it too, and prepared to cope with change.[2]

Such an aim suggests that in the upbringing of our children

we ought to have some concern for the following: certain skills (reading, writing and competence with computers) which have a functional value in a democratic community, are necessary means to further ends that the individual may one day choose to pursue, and, in the case of the first two, are importantly related to thinking; certain information which is important either functionally or in respect of a greater understanding of others and our community (history, literature and social study). Certain attitudes and behavioural patterns which both contribute to the successful working of a democracy and the ease with which the individual lives within it, and in some cases, enhance the values of democracy (tolerance, respect for others, respect for law, respect for knowledge and systematic reasoning, beneficence). Intellectual skills too will have an obvious value but I cannot see that words such as 'creativity', 'critical thinking', 'crap-detecting', or 'lateral thinking' add much to the basic concepts of a rational disposition and competence within a given sphere.

4.3 To meet the end outlined above I am proposing a compulsory common core curriculum consisting of the following: a primary stage (Grades 1-7) devoted to health and moral training, the development of numeracy and literacy, and exploring; a transition year (Grade 8) during which the natural sciences, mathematics and the fine arts are studied; and a secondary stage (Grades 9-12) devoted to the study of English, history, social study and, in the particular circumstances of Canada, French. But before elaborating on and explaining the particular curricular proposals, it is necessary to say something about the notion of a compulsory common core curriculum itself.

4.4 The term 'curriculum' refers to the content, in the sense of that which is overtly taught in the school. But, as we have seen, the radicals are clearly correct to draw our attention to the phenomenon of the hidden curriculum. The content of the hidden curriculum may or may not be consciously taught by the teachers. What distinguishes it is that it is not timetabled or otherwise advertised to the learner. Since there is a hidden curriculum, any proposed curriculum reform or planning must take account of the hidden curriculum too.

The proposal of a common *core* curriculum emphasizes that this curriculum should take up only a part of the typical school day; it is the core, which implies something crucial and central, of the upbringing process—it is by no means the whole of it. What I actually propose is that something like three hours of morning school each day should be devoted to this curriculum. For the rest I propose a totally voluntary situation such that children need not even attend school, if they do not wish it. But at the same time, I enjoin the school to have as wide-ranging a programme of organized activities as is practically possible (given teacher interest and competence, finance and locale) available and brought to the attention of pupils. These activities may range from chess to operating lathes and may, where possible, involve close co-operation with local industries and other sectors of the community. Of course, as things are, such proposals would not be easy to implement. But I nonetheless make the proposal for the following reasons: a) I do not know of any compelling argument to justify the amount of time and the amount of material that we currently demand in schools. To take one instance, I do not know of a convincing argument for all the time that so many children spend on the study of mathematics (once beyond the level of numeracy). b) In addition to that negative but strong reason, the radicals are surely correct in saying that we take school too seriously, to the point at which we only regard learning achieved in school as worthwhile or real. That is ridiculous, as we all appreciate as soon as we think about it. Many useful things may be learnt out of school, and it is a good thing in itself to stress that point by organizing schooling as if we believed it. c) The radicals are also correct in their perception that a little enthusiasm goes a long way (despite generally woefully overstating their case) and their various proposals about learning resources, learning webs and networks are in principle sensible. But they are characteristically overdone and unrealistic. It is not unrealistic to propose using the schools, which already exist, in line with radical ideas to a much greater extent.

4.5 By 'common' I mean common to all pupils. That is likely to be a pardonable exaggeration, since there are bound to be some children who are in one way or another unsuited to this curriculum and need special treatment. But, broadly speaking, I mean common to all students.

What is the argument for a common curriculum of any sort,

especially in a land as full of diversity as Canada? There are many arguments that tend in the same direction. I would like to draw attention to four of them.

1) *Argument from knowledge*. The extent to which the characterization of knowledge and its dissemination are culture free is open to debate. Nonetheless, as I have argued above, there are certain aspects of knowledge that are without question supra-cultural and not matters of subjective opinion. For example, the discipline of mathematics and the logical distinction between questions of the type "Is this painting popular?" and "Is this painting good?" Such distinctions are universal, common for all men and therefore belong equally to all men. Equally it is certain that knowledge and education are conceptually linked.[3] It has been suggested that not all communities necessarily share the view that education and knowledge are intimately linked, and the classical Spartans, who rejoiced in a very thorough military totalitarian state, have been cited as a case in point. But clearly the Spartans did not dissent from the view that education is about transmitting knowledge. It is rather that they had their own distinctive view of the nature of knowledge, so that we find it hard to appreciate that what they thought they were doing was handing down knowledge. If it is agreed that schools should be at least partly concerned with education, if education logically implies transmission of knowledge, and if knowledge is in some respects and to some extent objective and supra-cultural, it follows that there will be some content that ideally should be common to all students.

2) *Argument from culture (with a small 'c')*. There are many cultures in an anthropological sense, which is to say a descriptive sense that refers to styles and ways of life. Some would use the existence of such distinct cultures or subcultures as an argument for distinctive curricula and differential schooling. But a) unless some further premisses are introduced that line of reasoning will involve the naturalistic fallacy in assuming that

because a thing exists (in this case a specific culture) it is good that it should do so. Or perhaps such qualities as local colour, quaintness or anthropological value are being confused with inherent or educational value. The truth is, however, that in various specifiable ways some cultures are superior to others; in this context, where we are assuming a common aim it will sometimes be a matter of fairly straightforward demonstration to show that some features of some subcultures are better suited to achieving that aim than others. b) The fact that there are distinguishable subcultures in a community does not preclude the possibility that there is also a common culture. In all countries with which I am familiar, and this would include Canada, there clearly is a common culture as well as a network of subcultures. c) Most important of all is the contention that even if there were no common culture, we ought to develop and foster one. Communal life demands a common culture of some sort. People who have to live together and understand each other need common reference points.

There is no reason why a common curriculum should preclude some varying emphasis in the school on subcultural curriculum content, so there need not be any conflict here. All I wish to suggest is that the existence of distinct subcultures does not constitute an argument for various different curricula, and that schools should seek to provide some sort of common culture. At the simplest level they should make sure that we all drive on the same side of the road. At a higher level we must share expectations, see roles in the same sort of light and believe in the same sort of thing. Above all, we must believe in the way of life of our community including, in this instance, the democratic procedures of our nation.

3) *Argument from Culture (with a capital 'c')*. Here I refer to High Culture in T.S. Eliot's sense.[4] Culture in this sense is defined in terms of quality, as witness Matthew Arnold's phrase "the best that has been thought and said in the world."[5] Certainly there are problems about deciding on the criteria for determining the best (not to

mention the problems about applying such criteria and deciding what *is* best). But it is obviously a mistake to move from the observations that preferences may vary, that cultural influences may effect taste, and that there is a logical problem about the status of value judgments, directly to the conclusion that there are no such things as qualitative differences. We may argue about what *is* the best that has been spoken, but that does not mean that everything has been equally well said. Every activity carries within its description its own set of standards (or possibly, in some cases, sets of standards) and by those standards some examples of the activity in question are better than others. It seems undeniable that education is a normative concept and that it is by definition concerned with the worthwhile and with quality. The argument from Culture asserts that what is good in, say, the field of literature is not a function of who you are, but a function of what literature is, and that therefore concern for the best will once again point towards a common curriculum.

4) *Argument from choice*. Choice is conceptually bound up with the ideal of the autonomous-democratic man. To give people complete freedom of choice would be to give them complete knowledge of all alternatives and the means and ability to undertake all of them. (Choice in ignorance we call blind, which is to say no choice at all.) In practice, in a far from perfect situation, we have to adopt some strategy to increase choice as far as we may. We have to decide, for example, whether it is more beneficial, in terms of choice, to make many trivial options available to people or a few more complex ones. The argument I am now referring to holds that there are some activities that are both significant and complex: 'significant' in the sense of importantly related to the way of life of the society in question, as scientific understanding is and chess is not to our way of life; 'complex' in the sense of not being easily picked up or understood through mere description, looking on or brief acquaintanceship. In this sense sociology is more complex than football. Choice is increased in important

> ways, if people are brought to an understanding of those activities that are both significant and complex: doors are opened that are by definition hard to open, but worth opening.

4.6 That the common core curriculum should be compulsory follows from what has already been said. To argue for a common curriculum is to argue for its being compulsory. For if it is to be common for good reason, that is to say that all ought to do it. If all ought to do it, even if they do not want to, and if therefore all are going to do it, that is to say that it is compulsory.

'Compulsion' is however a dirty word; perhaps inevitably in that part of the hemisphere that calls itself 'free', it has evil connotations. We must face the fact, then, that compulsion does sometimes involve making people do things even when they do not want to and/or do not see the point of doing them. Compulsion entails demanding. A compulsory course is one that you are obliged to take; it implies that some form of sanction can, and will, be brought to bear on you if you do not do it. But compulsion does not necessarily involve or imply strong-arm stuff; it does not necessarily imply 'force' in the sense of violence, but only in the sense of some kind of sanction, and sanctions may take many forms. To say that something is compulsory, therefore, tells us that something has to be done, and that there is some kind of machinery to make sure that we do it. It does not necessarily imply anything about unpleasantness or brute force.

It should also be noted that, of course, to make something compulsory is not necessarily to suggest that people are reluctant to do it and will need to be constrained by sanctions. ("Compulsion does sometimes involve making people do things *even* when they do not want to", not 'although' or 'whenever'.) It is too often assumed that, if something is compulsory, it must be unpopular; that is obviously not necessarily so, since the fact that something is made compulsory need not imply reluctance on the part of those who are thus constrained. It does not preclude the possibility that those who are in fact under compulsion may also freely choose to do what they would otherwise be compelled to do. This is one point where the radical tradition has gone off the rails. The radicals' confused view of human nature and their hazy conception of reality lead them to the belief (or allow them to entertain this belief as well as any other) that there is an inevitable tension between what people 'naturally' want to do, and what the school expects them to do.[6] But the tension is not inevitable. Once it has been decided that something ought to be studied compulsorily, there are many ways in which the school can remove any taint of force, reluctance or unwillingness. The child can be interested; he can be led or guided, firmly but gently; he can be motivated by a variety of extraneous factors.

Finally it should be observed that talk of compulsion need imply nothing for the classroom situation. It is a common but quite unwarranted mistake to assume that commitment to a compulsory curriculum entails commitment to what are pejoratively termed 'traditional teaching methods.' In fact, such commitment carries with it no methodological implications whatsoever. Attendance at an orgy might be compulsory.

That concludes what I wish to say about the principle of a compulsory common curriculum. I shall now return to my specific curriculum proposals.

4.7 The primary stage consists of an overt curriculum concerned with developing literacy, numeracy, computer competency, physical health and 'exploring'. Despite the objection of some, such as Paul Goodman,[7] that the value of functional literacy has been overdone, it is surely clear that the following points combined make an overwhelming case for its importance: 1) It *does* have a functional value; that is to say it is useful to be able to read notices, write letters, read newspapers. 2) It is a *sine qua non* of so many further activities which, whatever their inherent value, the individual may want to be in a position to choose whether to pursue. 3) Writing is one medium of expression, but it differs from others such as speaking in that it is easier to control, modify and correct. It is therefore a very good medium for *improving* people's power of expression. Numeracy is to be defended in terms of the first two points. Computer competency is going to be important for the next generation because so much will be done by computers. Not to understand them will place one at a practical disadvantage and render one alienated from the central feature of the age. Physical health is of obvious value. Some would argue, as against the classical tradition of a sound mind in a sound body, that promoting health is not part of education. Very likely not, but it should be part of the responsibility of the schools, if we see them as concerned with the upbringing of children who may become autonomous and democratic citizens. The final element in the overt curriculum is what I call 'exploring'. The point of using that term is to divorce us from any associative ideas that terms such as 'creativity', 'biology', or 'social studies' may have, and to make it clear that I see no case for, and do not propose, the systematic study, on however low a level, of such things as chemistry. Provided that the vital elements already referred to are catered for, the emphasis to be found in the radical tradition on sustaining and promoting interest in, fascination for and enthusiasm for our surroundings is surely to be welcomed. I am therefore proposing that such time as is available (within the compulsory timetable) should be devoted to exploring the world about the child. Two points: much of this exploration may be local, but the radicals are surely mistaken in laying all stress on the local. In order to forge points of reference, to increase awareness and interest, to enlarge the potential scope for choice, and to lay the foundations of knowledge and universals, exploration should include both that which transcends time and place (e.g., exploration of natural phenomena) and that which is non-local (e.g., exploration of other localities, of museums, of government offices).

This completes the overt curriculum. I do not envisage lessons in morality or values clarification.[8] There is no evidence whatsoever that individuals become more moral, in the specific sense of more inclined to abide by moral values, as a result of so-called moral education programmes. There is a lot of evidence, however, that the job can be well done through the hidden curriculum. I therefore propose a return to the unashamed use of the hidden curriculum as the medium of moral upbringing. In other words, I propose that teachers and the school system itself should deliberately foster the specific attitudes and values referred to above (e.g., tolerance, impartiality, concern for well-being of others, respect for persons) by the time-honoured means of example, praise and blame, and expectation and homily. The hidden curriculum should also foster concern for non-moral values, such as health, industry and rationality.

I have argued thus for many years and here in particular I am accused (as if it mattered) of being unoriginal. I could go further: in the present climate I am being, in a purely descriptive sense, reactionary. But my reasons are clear: no coherent case can be made against the morality of this procedure; no coherent case can be made for the effectiveness of values-education programmes; it is absolutely clear, indeed that is why the radicals object to it, that the hidden curriculum *can* do the job, and very effectively. Witness classical Sparta, the English Public School, Maoist China, the Samoans, or the Russian system. The last in particular furnishes a useful example in view of Urie Bronfenbrenner's research into the comparative styles of upbringing of the U.S.A. and U.S.S.R., published as *Two Worlds of Childhood*,[9] which clearly establishes what is anyway intuitively to be expected: the Russians as a result of their upbringing have a clear commitment to a coherent set of values. Many Americans do not.

4.8 The transitional year is something special. In general I see no case for making all individuals study the natural sciences, mathematics and the fine arts. As I have argued in *Common Sense and the Curriculum* there is no convincing case to show that they ought to: they will not necessarily be the better for it in any identifiable way; they will not be the worse for it if they do not.[10]

But that is not to say that these subjects are worthless. On the contrary, given broadly our way of life and our ideal, it is very important that we continue to produce skilled scientists and mathematicians and that the fine arts are not stifled, reserved for the few or made to serve some ideology. The argument for their inclusion as compulsory subjects for one year, and one year only, is that they are paradigm examples of pursuits that are both significant and complex. So complex are they, that few would ever approach them or conceive that they might be of interest to them, unless they had at some stage been initiated into them and brought to some understanding of what the activities involve. Having been compelled to go into the water, individuals may decide for themselves, now or later, whether they want to swim about. These subjects will continue to be available as voluntary options in the secondary stage.

4.9 The secondary stage involves the compulsory study of English, history, social study and French. The argument for the last is peculiar to Canada. In Britain, where it is more or less compulsory to study French for many years, I know of no convincing argument for that demand. But in a country, so long as it wishes to remain one country, that contains two large populations speaking a different language, the objective of a harmonious and effective democracy would seem to suggest that both populations should acquire facility in the language of the other, partly as a mark of mutual respect, partly to provide access to some of the culture of either community, and partly to facilitate communication on a political and an everyday level.

By social study, I mean study of anything pertaining to the society in question, in practical terms the most significant elements or features of that society. It is under this heading that much of the common culture referred to above will be introduced: information about customs, education, the distribution of wealth, treatment of the elderly, delinquency, the police and religion. The stress falls on providing *information* about society, not on going through the embryonic motions of being a sociologist, being initiated into a religion, theorizing about causes or moralizing about consequences. I call it 'social study' rather than 'social studies' to indicate that the emphasis falls on studying society and not on varying methods of study. The object is that future generations shall be a great deal better informed about their society than most of us are. Such information is a necessary prerequisite of rational-democratic behaviour and approaching the ideal we have in mind.

Having mentioned religion I will permit myself a brief aside on the matter. The practice of religious assemblies in schools constitutes a particular facet of the hidden curriculum, a facet which is very often bolstered in many other little ways in schools. I have argued above that there is nothing inherently wrong with the phenomenon of the hidden curriculum and have advocated its use in respect of moral upbringing. However there is no obvious case to justify the covert (or overt) influencing towards religious belief that schools sometimes engage in, as there is to justify the fostering of moral values. The need for some kind of moral code in order to maintain society remains whatever the logical status of moral propositions. But that need has not been established in the case of religion: there is no logical connection between morality and religion and there is no empirical evidence that I know of to establish the truth of the cliché that men need to believe in religion in order to behave morally. Time and again the basic postulates of religion have been shown to be quite unprovable one way or the other: they involve conjecture that deliberately places itself beyond rational assessment. That does not establish that such postulates are necessarily false, but it does mean that in the final analysis there is no more reason to believe in them than the postulates of witchcraft. But religion in the widest sense, being a significant phenomenon compared with the latter (which may at best be a small part of religion), does deserve to be noted with some care in the course of social study.

The argument for the compulsory study of English and history is essentially bound up with a particular view of what such study should involve. I do not mean specifically the study of accredited great works of literature, although some thought must be paid to such works, given the Culture considerations outlined above. Nor, more importantly, do I mean conscious study of literary technique or aesthetic considerations. Likewise with history, I do not primarily intend to suggest a concern for developing good historians. In terms of the overt curriculum, the main point or feature of the study I propose in history and literature is a concern for content. I am suggesting selecting and using that content for the following purposes: to give ideas; to promote awareness of differences and possibilities; to promote understanding of how things have come about, how accidental such origins may be and how different they might be.

At the same time the hidden curriculum content of such courses can include the intellectual virtues of concern for evidence, precision, and imagination.

I have in the past argued for a further stage of education involving philosophy.[11] In view of what I mean by philosophy, it now seems to me that the same purpose would be better achieved by insisting that the study of English, history and social study gradually beomes more philosophical: that is to say (in my understanding of the term) that discussion, writing, argument and any other form of activity relating to the material should increasingly be concerned with clarity of meaning, making fine distinctions (particularly distinguishing different kinds of questions) and coherence and precision of argument.

I shall have more to say on the precise nature of the English and history courses that I propose in the next chapter. For the moment the reasoning behind this essentially arts, and not very extensive, curriculum should be clear enough. It is designed to produce people who are well informed about their society, aware of its accidental quality and open-minded to alternatives, linked by the sense and the actuality of a common culture, and disposed to consider matters rationally. There is a view to the effect that if one wants autonomous and democratic adults one must give autonomy and democracy to children. But it is likely that this view is based upon the confusion between defining and generative criteria that was noted above in reference to the radicals. Sometimes the two coincide: we define a cripple by reference to a damaged leg, and we may generate cripples by damaging people's legs. But sometimes they do not. It is true that part of the definition of autonomy is that the individual does as he sees fit; true too that democracy involves participation. But it clearly does not follow that one necessarily produces autonomous democratic citizens by leaving people alone as children, that it would be sufficient to do so. In fact, given the definitions of the terms outlined above, it is clear that taking certain specific steps, such as cultivating the attitudes, developing the skills and providing the information referred to, will enhance the likelihood of achieving the aim. The ultimate aim certainly demands some kind of open methodology of teaching during the final years of the secondary stage, but in the earlier stages the important thing is to get the information, the skills and the attitudes across, by whatever means prove most effective for particular teachers in particular situations.

4.10 Notwithstanding my comments above, some will say that the programme I have outlined is not eduation so much as schooling, socialization or indoctrination. I am inclined to respond by asking "What does it matter what it is called?" I have explained what it involves and given my reasons for advocating it. But I had better say a little more. I take education to be initiation into culture and knowledge and the provision of understanding of "the reason why of things".[12] Therefore taken as a whole this is an educational programme. It is, of course, true that the programme also involves schooling (taking that as something akin to training) and socialization, and at certain given moments the individual is strictly speaking neither undergoing education nor has he been educated. But that is justified by appeal to the consideration that schools are concerned with various aspects of upbringing and not just education, and very properly so, because various types of training and socialization are necessary to our ideal and/or as a means towards the emergence of the educated man.

This programme certainly does not constitute indoctrination as I would define it—namely as the deliberate inculcation of belief with the intention that that belief will not be ousted, come what may—nor in any other sense that would make indoctrination necessarily repugnant.[13] It is not indoctrination in the sense given, because the intention is to produce the very reverse of the closed mind. The idea is that in the end the individual shall be autonomous. It is true that in order to facilitate that end, I propose early stages of habituation, socialization and training. That seems to me right, proper and necessary, particularly given the aim in question. But, in fact, some such procedure would seem to be advisable for any state; for any state must seek to bring up citizens who will not find the terms of life within it too irksome or too alien.

I have referred above to the mistaken view that theory and practice can be easily divorced.[14] That this kind of theorizing is relevant to practice is self-evident. Assuming that it is coherent, it amounts to an explanation of why we should be doing certain specific things.

But it is, of course, true that practice will not be altered solely as a result of educationalists theorizing. What is to go on, it may be thought, is actually determined by the Ministry, the Board of Education, the headmaster or principal—anybody, in fact, except the teacher who shrugs his shoulders and says "so teach me how to teach what I've got to teach; don't speculate on what I ought to teach." The truth is however that what happens is the outcome of a spiralling interplay between thought and action. Things will not change at once just because someone argues for a change. But certainly nothing will change except in so far as people are prepared to entertain alternative ideas and arguments—in short to think about the nature of the enterprise in which they are engaged.

Notes

1. My definition of "democratic" is of course stipulative. For further discussion of the concept of autonomy, see my *Moral Philosophy for Education*, op. cit., ch. 8, p. 131.
2. Radicals such as Postman, Weingartner and Toffler are surely correct in seeing ubiquitous change as a significant characteristic of our age.
3. The literature on this topic is extensive. For the seminal statement of the matter, see R. S. Peters, *Ethics and Education*, London: George Allen and Unwin Ltd., 1966, part 1.
4. T. S. Eliot, *Notes Towards the Definition of Culture*, London: Faber and Faber Ltd., 1968.
5. Matthew Arnold, *Literature and Dogma*, New York: Macmillan and Co., 1895, preface p. xxvii.
6. See above, ch. 3.
7. "Freedom and Learning: the need for choice" in *The Curriculum: Context, Design and Development*, op. cit., p. 110.
8. On values clarification see below, ch. 5.
9. Urie Bronfenbrenner, *Two Worlds of Childhood, U.S. and U.S.S.R.*, New York: Russell Sage Foundation, 1970.
10. *Common Sense and the Curriculum*, op. cit., ch. 4.
11. Ibid.
12. The phrase is used by R. S. Peters whose views on the concept of education I closely follow. See his *Ethics and Education*, op. cit.
13. See R. G. Woods and R. Barrow, *An Introduction to the Philosophy of Education*, op. cit., ch. 4.
14. See above ch. 1.3.

CHAPTER 5

Classroom Practice

5.1 In this chapter I wish to move from the general curricular considerations of the last chapter to more specific classroom issues, and to address myself to the problem of converting those requirements into practice. I shall examine in more detail what will be involved in teaching English and history and consider the question of whether there are any methodological implications in the preceding argument.

Certain features of my proposals can be highlighted by comparing them with the superficially similar current Ontario provisions. The similarity *is* only superficial, however. Even a logistical comparison reveals important differences. Thus in a four year period the Ontario Ministry demands 2,420 hours of compulsory school attendance from the child; 1,650 of those hours are devoted to activities or studies which no particular individual *has* to engage in, but which are nonetheless thought to be so important that everybody ought to do some of them. Such an attitude to an activity is not necessarily illogical or contradictory. But it does require some kind of framework of ideas whereby it is justified. On the face of it, that is lacking in the Ministry's proposals. By contrast, my proposals demand only 1,650 hours of compulsory attendance all told, and all that time is devoted to pursuits, the importance of which is such that all who can should engage in them. More specifically, my proposals involve spending double the time on English (440 hours as opposed to 220) and half the time on mathematics (110 hours as opposed to 220). In addition my proposals involve 440 hours devoted to social study and 440 hours devoted to history—the nearest comparison to that in the Ontario programme is the 220 hour Canadian studies course. Both programmes require 110 hours of science, though for rather different reasons. Finally, I include 110 hours devoted to the fine arts.

Taken all in all and judged from the perspective of the actual child and his everyday experience that amounts to a big difference between the two programmes. Ideally, as already indicated, I would also argue for total freedom for the child during the rest of the day; but I can see the practical difficulties in the idea of releasing children from school completely for most of the day and I accept that for the time being the school will have to continue playing the role of child-custodian. Given that, it seems clear that we should concentrate on equipping the schools with a wide range of resources on which the children may freely draw when not engaged in the compulsory curriculum. I have in mind resources such as boats, vehicles to transport them to water, mountaineering equipment, libraries, motor-mechanic shops—resources that represent the world as it is rather than the childlike collection of slides, tapes and records that usually clutter up the school resource centre. The kinds of resources I have in mind require substantial funding, of course, but it is here that such money as is available should be channelled, rather than into new buildings, teaching aids or teachers' salaries.

The differences in compulsory attendance time demanded by the Ontario programme and mine are, so to speak, the qualitative embodiment of the differing rationale that lies behind each curriculum and the differing emphasis laid on the importance of the school as such in the child's upbringing. In addition to those differences of time there are also, as will have been noted, certain clear differences of content. Study of the fine arts is not compulsory in Ontario at any stage, for example. Conversely, there is a pronounced emphasis on the compulsory study of Canadiana (by which term I signify the whole range of Canadian studies options). But mention of Canadiana brings me on to the main focus of difference, which lies in what I and the Ministry respectively mean by some of these terms. It is by now a well worn commonplace that even the compulsory elements of the Ontario programme do not necessarily constitute a common core curriculum, since the vagueness of the Ministry guidelines gives individual schools considerable latitude and the variety that that engenders is reinforced by the system of school, as opposed to external provincial, examinations. Consequently, what the Ministry means by English, what happens in practice in various schools and what I mean by English may vary considerably and constitute the most marked difference between my proposals and current Ontario practice. I shall therefore now look in more detail at English, history, social study, Canadian studies and fine arts as curriculum subjects.

5.2 *English.*
Three interesting things emerge from the recent Hall-Carlton report in respect of English. First, the enrolment for English (and mathematics) courses did not decline with the curriculum innovations of the last ten years, as may be popularly supposed. Consequently, there can be no simple cause and effect relationship between a more open curriculum and any alleged drop in skills associated with the study of English. Secondly, the report anyway finds "no evidence of any meaningful relationship between English credits and skill adequacy in either reading or writing".[1] Thirdly, there is widespread agreement amongst the sample canvassed that a) there has been a decline of some sort in respect of certain allegedly specifiable skills, and b) English has become "a forum for the exploration of social and cultural issues"[2] rather than a means of improving communication skills. All of that adds up to the message that we had better establish what we mean by and what we want from the study of English.

Perhaps the General Aims of the Ministry Curriculum Guideline (Intermediate Division) are rather ambitious and far-flung, but they do include unambiguous reference to the importance of language proficiency in both oral and written form. (See Figure 1)

The first stated aim is slightly grandiose and obscure; it puts the stress on language as a means to developing various quasi-moral characteristics such as initiative and integrity. The second aim refers to its use as a means to becoming acquainted with various aspects of Canadiana. The third and seventh refer to the goal of appreciating literature as an art form. But the fourth and fifth aims put the emphasis squarely

Figure 1. Statement of Aims in Ontario English Curriculum Guideline for the Intermediate Division.[3]

GENERAL AIMS

1. To encourage the use of language as a means by which the individual understands personal and societal goals and acquires such qualities as initiative, responsibility, decisiveness, self-discipline, perceptiveness and integrity in the pursuit of those goals;
2. to nurture the student's growth in awareness and appreciation of both personal identity and the diverse values of people as reflected in Canada's multicultural society and literature;
3. to promote the student's appreciation and enjoyment of literature and language;
4. to develop language proficiency by increasing the student's conscious understanding and practical application of the principles and processes by which language operates;
5. to increase the student's general use and mastery of language by developing the particular language skills required throughout the curriculum;
6. to familiarize the student with representative contemporary and classical works and the various literary genres;
7. to develop the student's critical skills and help him apply them in responding to material transmitted through the various media.

on developing the student's capacity to use and understand language to good purpose as a means of communication. One oversimplified way of summarizing the intent of the General Aims is to say that they call for both the development of literary sensibility in the widest sense (a sensibility to literature and a sensibility derived from literature) and the development of rationality or critical thinking. (The seventh aim, indeed, talks of developing "the student's critical skills", apparently without reference to any particular context.) Thus we are told that "language is a process intimately linked with personal growth and the human need for communication".[4] Most of the Guideline introduction in fact lays the stress on the value of vicarious experience and the aim of developing sensibility. But the balance is somewhat redressed by the list of objectives, which is preponderantly cognitive, perhaps because it is assumed that it is more feasible to measure success in the student's ability to understand an argument than to measure the success of his appreciation of something. The emphasis on communication is also evident when it is stated that the role of the English teacher includes a proclivity to use "precise and effective English". The programme as a whole should involve "an integrated balance of reading, writing, speaking and listening".[5]

What are we to say to all this? Before we say anything other than that it looks a pretty ambitious programme with which we do not appear to be having spectacular success, we need to look more closely at three key terms: 'communication', 'composition' and 'literature'.

5.3 The term 'communication' crops up repeatedly in Canadian educational literature, almost always without qualification or elaboration, despite the fact that there are clearly different senses of 'communication'. Four spring immediately to mind.

1) Some people mean by the ability to communicate the ability to get on with people easily. This is the sense in which the financial community of Albertown understand the term. When they judge the school-leaver as a potential clerk in the bank in respect of his competence in oral communication, they look to see whether he has an agreeable personality. No doubt agreeable personalities are agreeable; perhaps too the study of English grammar and/or literature may contribute to the development of such a personality. But it hardly seems that communication in this sense can be the justification for a course in English.[6]

2) There are allegedly a number of kinds of communication that are non-rational.[7] Many of these are also non-verbal. For example, people talk of telepathetic communication or of communicating ideas through music or painting. But there are also, or so it might be claimed, non-rational verbal forms of communication. Some poetry, it might be argued, speaks or communicates something which cannot be equated with the descriptive content. I am not here referring to the obvious point that words and phrases have connotations or associative ideas that may vary for different people and therefore alter the overall impact of a given poem. I am talking of the suggestion that some literature communicates only through its form. Its message is in no way subject to rational analysis.

That there may be some such literature, as there surely is some such art in other areas, I do not dispute. The question is what we can say about it, when the premiss is that it is non-rational, whereas what we say about things to each other is, hopefully, cast in the rational mood. At any rate, we must distinguish between two suggestions: the suggestion that it is possible to have non-rational understanding of certain things, particularly art forms, and the suggestion that such a form of understanding can be used to help us to communicate with each other in something like sense 4 below. The former suggestion is a reference to what, to avoid further confusion, I shall call 'aesthetic appreciation', and there is undoubtedly such a thing. Furthermore 'aesthetic appreciation' may bring people together, just as an interest in fishing might. But developing an 'aesthetic appreciation' has no more to do with increasing communication (sense 4) than developing an interest in fishing has.

3) The next two senses are very closely related but nonetheless distinct. The difference lies in the fact that the first uses the term 'communication' in a neutral way, the second regards it as normative. It is a difference comparable to the neutral use of 'rational', as in "man is a rational animal", and the normative use, as in "he is a rational man; I wish you were". One can talk about developing an individual's capacity to communicate and mean no more than that one is developing his ability to convey ideas, suggestions, wants, and opinions to other people and to understand those of others. No reference is made to the quality of either the ideas conveyed or the quality of the manner in which they are conveyed. In this neutral sense communication would be achieved whenever two people of similar background and communicative ability can understand each other. In this sense two chimpanzees may communicate as well as two human beings and very likely better than some.

It should be at once apparent that communication in this sense is not enough. If all we were concerned about was that children should acquire the ability to communicate in a neutral sense, there would, in most cases, be no need for school at all. People will learn to communicate in this sense in their peer group and in their family.

4) The fourth sense of communication is a normative variant of the third. What we wish to develop is the ability to communicate (sense 3) well. The question is therefore what is it to communicate well? It is, at the very least, to have at one's command a range of precise and detailed concepts, a wide range of differing and strange concepts, and a talent for their coherent and logical organization. More briefly it is the facility to express oneself clearly and coherently and to make sharp discriminations. The mastery of a language, which will be the medium of communication, is a question of seeing and expressing distinctions. It is not just a matter of symbols. If you don't know the Latin word *amicitia* then you lack one of many verbal symbols for friendship. That doesn't matter. But it does matter if you lack the ability to distinguish between different kinds of friendship—if you have only one concept or idea of friendship. What is desirable is to increase one's capacity to make subtle distinctions about friendship (or anything else). To communicate well requires a rich array of concepts.

Literature may be studied for many purposes of which the following four would seem as important as any. (I am not suggesting that it can only be studied for one of these purposes at a time.)

1) It can be studied as an art form or in aesthetic terms. This would involve concern for such technical matters as the form of a novel, the organization of material, the evocative tendency of the whole.
2) It can be studied primarily as a repository of ideas or for what it says. In this case it is a vehicle for its content.
3) It can be studied for what it reveals about human interaction, motivation and intention. This is part of its con-

tent, but it is content of a particular and subtle kind which is generally covertly conveyed at the same time as other overt themes are handled.

4) It can be studied as a model of composition.

Usually, these purposes are inextricably interwoven. The medium is to some extent the message: the manner of writing shapes the ideas. Nonetheless in principle such distinctions can be made, and it is important that they should be, since there are possible alternative ways of serving some of the purposes. For instance, written literature studied for the first three purposes alone faces a serious challenge from good television drama. At the present time there is not a great deal of the latter, certainly nothing to compare with the accumulated literary heritage of the world. But there are sufficient examples to indicate that this medium can equally effectively be imbued with artistic purpose and can prove equally effective in disseminating ideas. For practical reasons it may generally be less inclined to discourse on intrapersonal themes but it may still treat of them successfully. We have to face the fact that for many purposes there is nothing necessarily inferior about a television production of a great novel. In fact, the only purpose of study that could not be met in any way other than by study of literature is the purpose of studying it as a model of composition.[8]

By composition I mean writing with a view to communicating in sense 4 above. Writing not to display one's mood or feelings, not for aesthetic purpose, not in the service of mysticism—but writing for the purpose of expressing oneself succinctly, sharply, clearly and coherently. Writing rationally.

5.4 What of the relationship between writing and thinking? All too often we hear remarks like "I can't put my case on paper very well, but I have it in my mind." Now, assuming that the speaker doesn't lack a pen, have some physical disability or a psychological horror of putting pen to paper, what on earth can he mean? What does he mean when he says that his case is in his mind? Presumably, he means that he can articulate that case to himself. In what medium does he talk to himself, if not in words? Then why cannot he write them down? The truth is that if, for reasons other than the sort referred to above, you cannot articulate your case on paper, then you cannot do so in your mind. Those who write badly, think badly. Those who write well, think well.

Having said that, we need to delineate the important aspects of good writing. It seems clear that we should distinguish between spelling, punctuation and syntax. Such things as spelling and certain aspects of grammar (e.g., "whom I love" rather than "who I love") seem more to do with appearance than substance. If they are totally neglected, the language becomes incomprehensible to others; and, from a hidden curriculum point of view, there may be some value in causing students to worry about such things in order to develop a concern for appearances. The fact remains that in itself, within bounds, poor spelling and poor grammar of this sort do not impede communication. Punctuation is slightly different: there is nothing sacrosanct about it, certainly; our rules of punctuation are to some extent and our symbols of punctuation are altogether arbitrary. But most of what punctuation does is an integral part of the meaning of what we write. The difference between "the man, who . . ." and "the man who . . ." is a difference in meaning. The ability to punctuate correctly in either case is not just the ability to throw arbitrary symbols about: it is the ability to recognize two related but distinct ideas. When it comes to syntax we are heavily involved in meaning and the means of understanding and expressing. I include in syntax the framework of different kinds of clauses, moods, tenses, copulatives, conjunctions, etc. If you are oblivious of the difference between a consequential "so that" and a final "in order that", you lack something of the same order as he who confuses correlation and cause. (I should add that just as the demand for logical thought does not necessarily imply the study of formal logic, so the demand for concern with syntax does not necessarily imply the need to study syntax formally. It is not using the labels "consequential" and "final" clauses that matters, it is recognizing the difference between "he did this in order to kill him" and "he did this so that he killed him.")

5.5 I am arguing, then, that the teaching of English should concentrate on improving communication (sense 4), rationality being more immediately important than self-expression, creativity or aesthetic appreciation, if our aim is the development of autonomy or if using "precise and effective English" is our objective. Given that, we should select literature (which could be foreign literature in translation) with a view to its potentiality for stretching children a little bit in feeding them ideas (overt and covert content) and introducing them to new and more subtle distinctions, and with a view to its quality as a model of composition. On these terms Henry James is a better candidate for senior grade students than Agatha Christie or Arthur Hailey because James has a more discriminating perception of the world and the ability to communicate it to us; he makes us see things that we did not see before. He literally increases our understanding. (It should be noted that this is not a matter of cultural preference or subjective judgement. It may well be that some people think Hailey a better novelist than James; I certainly prefer reading Agatha Christie to either of them. But it is a matter of fact that neither Hailey nor Christie is as good as James *judged by the criteria in question*.) Naturally, the study of the material, once selected, should concern itself less with the aesthetic domain (e.g., questions about how effects are achieved) than with matters related to communication (e.g., how clarity and precision are obtained).

The teaching of composition should be the other main element in the English course. At the present time, writing is by far the most easily controlled form of expression. Though the study of literature may teach things that are essential to good communication, practice and correction are equally necessary. The written word can be examined, altered, compared and discussed and thus a real study of the best way of expressing something or the nature of what can be expressed can be made. The written form of expression is one of the best means of improving the spoken form, which is effectively one with the business of thinking.

5.6 In the previous paragraphs I have pushed aesthetic considerations aside. That is partly because of the greater importance of seeing English as a vehicle for the teaching of communication and partly because there seems no reason to confine the aesthetic to the domain of literature. The transition year involves initiating children into the aesthetic dimensions of music, painting and sculpture as well as literature. The aesthetic dimension has its origin in the nature of these various activities. It may indeed go beyond them. At scattered but great moments in history something may go so far beyond the accepted norms of the activity as to redefine its nature. But generally speaking appreciating music, literature and other art forms as art forms begins in understanding their nature. Consequently our task is to help students master the basic language of the art forms in question or to understand what they are and what they involve.

5.7 I turn now to social study, history and the vexed question of Canadiana. One must distinguish here between the subject matter and the discipline—between trying to produce social scientists or historians and providing social or historical information. I certainly do not oppose the hope that we may encourage and enable students to become masters of their disciplines. And I certainly do advocate understanding and concern for reason and evidence at all times. Nonetheless, as I hope I have made clear, my argument for the compulsory study of history and social study is of such a sort that it follows that the emphasis in these studies should be on purveying information. The source of the evidence and any problems in the evidence should be considered wherever appropriate (that is a part of proper understanding and accurate information) but it is both unrealistic and irrelevant to our objectives to try to produce the scholar. Information has taken a real beating of late in educational discourse, largely because it is associated with specific old fashioned styles of teaching. But, in fact, it has no necessary connection with any style of teaching. I have referred to "exploring" in the primary stage, which term was deliberately used to imply the opposite of rote-learning and instruction, and yet the object of exploring is the gathering of information. The time has come to draw attention to how ignorant even quite sophisticated people often are in this basic sense: they are ill-informed about the nature of their society and how to operate within it. Worse, they are sometimes misinformed and unaware of how little they know.

The social study I propose should a) pertain for the most part to Canada b) involve comparison c) include such geographic information as is pertinent. Of course, there must be an emphasis on the country the students live in and have to cope with, and of course there are some geographical facts that are important. But the heavy emphasis on geography in the Ontario curriculum seems unwarranted on any terms and specifically not justified on mine.[9] The crucial thing is the comparative aspect. In the first place, we need to have some kind of international perspective in an international world. The nation is not self-sufficient and is not insulated against all manner of outside influences. Its citizens cannot afford to imagine that it is. In the second place, comparison informs information: that this is the way we do such and such is a great deal more significant once it is realized that somebody else does it another way. In the third place, it is important to inject a degree of the outward-looking attitude in students in order to feed the imagination, engender ideas and stimulate the mind against complacency. Social study, taught with an eye on these criteria can make a solid contribution towards the basic social awareness that effective democracy requires.

5.8 I do not see the study of history as a means of solving Canada's apparent crisis of identity. As to that I think there is a lot of conceptual confusion about what an identity is: the very idea of self-consciously seeking out (or is it attempting to create?) one's identity by studying oneself and one's works seems to me to be something approaching a nonsense. Identities grow with people; they become what people become, as a result of interaction between what the people were before and what they have experienced. The less the individual looks about him, beyond himself, the less interesting the self he develops; the more he engages in introspection at the expense of looking out, the more impoverished the identity that emerges. A sense of identity, one suspects, is not found by looking for it. So I resist the heavy emphasis on Canadiana that some would like to see in history and literature courses. I also incidentally question the unquestioned assumption that Canadian history starts in this country (and therefore isn't very rich or interesting) and that Canadian literature has to be defined as a new tradition defined by the subject matter of this country or birthplace of the author (and therefore isn't very good). It may be asserted that all things must have a beginning and unless there is a self-conscious effort to create Canadian culture now there never will be such a thing. But the evidence is against that view. Many civilizations have risen to greatness and produced their own cultural heritage on the backs of other cultures, as the Romans did on the Greeks. The Romans, who tried to resist the foreign influence, like Cato, lived on as quaint ostriches. Those who embraced and frankly took over true quality whatever its origin became the great Roman artists—men like Virgil and Horace. It is difficult to see how myopic sterility will not increase in more or less equal proportion to the emphasis placed on Canadiana. On this topic I cannot do better than quote again the oft-quoted remark of Morley Callaghan: "Forget all about the words 'identity' and 'culture', just never mention them. Seek only excellence and in good time people all over the world will ask about Canadians."[10]

Naturally the study of history must include reference to the history of the growth and development of the Canadian nation itself. But, to give point to that it must do more, and, to contribute to the ideal we have in mind, history must be regarded as something other than a way of coming to "an understanding of the Canadian identity" and certainly not invested with the quasi-moral purpose of developing "a reasoned pride in Canada" or burdened with the task of nurturing "an understanding of civic responsibility".[11] History should be comparative history and as wide ranging in time and place as is practically possible. It must be studied for its content, its ideas, in such a way as to promote awareness of differences and possibilities, and understanding of how things have come to be as they are and that they might have been otherwise. It must be used to enlarge horizons, to shake complacency, to stir the imagination. Only thus are the objectives met. To the question "But don't you care about developing civic responsibility, integrity, understanding what justice is and nurturing self-awareness and reasoned pride?" I reply: "I care about what I take to lie behind those words and phrases, but (at any rate until the concepts are considerably clarified) to propose them as the aims of teaching history is to become intolerably vague and comically overambitious. Nobody ever became a better citizen by studying history. What we can hope for is that some will become better informed and more open-minded about political life in the widest sense, and that is a necessary, albeit far from sufficient, condition of the autonomous and democratic citizen."

5.9 To summarize: in comparison with the current educational provisions in Ontario, I am proposing less time spent in the classroom, but more of that time spent on a compulsory core curriculum. I am arguing for an end to the conscious study of

Canadiana as such and a withdrawal from the heavy reliance placed on intellectual disciplines to develop moral and patriotic characteristics. My positive proposals involve increased emphasis on information about this society and the rest of the world, attention being paid to basic instruction in the realm of fine arts, and more concern for developing the power of communication in the sense outlined above.

5.10 These proposals carry with them very few implications for methodology. The 'exploring' in the elementary stage must by definition involve a relatively open school setting, conversely the hidden curriculum programme of moral upbringing presupposes that some forms of behaviour will be actively discouraged. At the secondary level the overall concern for precision and fine discrimination will lead to some attention being paid to detail and accuracy in all activities, while the aim of autonomy demands that toward the end of schooling at least students should be encouraged and enabled to exhibit autonomous behaviour. But for the most part nothing about teaching methods is presupposed: that literacy is a goal of the elementary stage is not to say that any particular approach, from formal to informal, is to be recommended. It is quite logical to argue that something *must* be taught, but to add that the best way to teach it is in an informal and unstructured setting. Conversely something might not be particularly worth teaching, unless students happened to express interest in it, but might nonetheless be of such a sort that, if it were to be taught, it would best be taught by very formal methods. When it comes to discussing teaching methodology there is a tendency for people to talk and act as if they were defending or abusing some religious doctrine. That is to say people believe fanatically in one thing or another and regard variant or different views as little short of heresy. It is safe to say that this impassioned attitude to the inquiry method, instruction, audio-visual aids or whatever it may be is quite unwarranted. There is no research on this matter that unambiguously establishes anything. The most recent research in Britain, a study by Neville Bennett, has been hailed by some as evidence for the superiority of traditional methods over progressive methods.[12] I don't think it does show that; if anything it shows that it is practically impossible to hold enough variables constant to establish anything. But it certainly does indicate that there is no warrant for claiming that there is an identifiable set of progressive methods which are necessarily superior. It is one of the fallacies of our age to believe that because teaching methods can be physically observed in a way that, say, the aim of teaching for democracy cannot, it follows that methodological issues fall in the realm of hard fact and can be settled decisively and scientifically. But practically every step in that chain of reasoning is confused and invalid. Teaching methods are not uncontentious, autonomous and easily identifiable items to be handed around to experts for examination. Interpretations of what, say, instruction is may vary considerably, and it is worth noting that the term is unlikely to be used in a value-free way. But even if it were the case that instances of instruction were as easy to pick out as motor cars, it would no more follow that claims about its efficacy and value could be settled decisively than it does that all arguments about the superiority of one car over another can be brought to an end. The idea that the sort of research that goes on into teaching methods is truly scientific is a gross distortion, since in the nature of things it cannot compare with the model of the physical sciences, where variables can be controlled and specimens cannot be self-conscious. Above all the idea that methodological research (which might fairly be characterized as systematic observation, sometimes in quasi-controlled situations) is necessarily more reliable or objective than other kinds of inquiry into other sorts of educational issue is sheer nonsense. Work like that of Richard Peters on the concept of education, for all its imperfections, tells us far more that is more or less certainly true about what educators should be trying to do, than most empirical research has been able to tell us.[13] One of the great myths of our time must be exploded: empirical research does not necessarily furnish more facts than pure reflection. That being the case it seems legitimate to risk the following a *priori* claims:

a) A variety of teaching methods may prove successful, success being related to such diverse factors as the individual, the age-group, and the subject-matter in question. It is likely that there is something in itself to be said for using a variety of styles.

b) *Contra* the radicals, interest can certainly be created and promoted.
c) Again *contra* the radical thesis, learning can take place by way of drills and instruction.
d) There is no clear evidence, and it is not necessarily true, that a free or open situation leads to the development of creative, open or critical minds in any obviously desirable sense of those words.
e) It is not demonstrable that the discipline of a subject demands a disciplined approach in the classroom in any obvious and meaningful sense of 'disciplined'.
f) But it is likely that a secure foundation in a subject will, in most cases, be most readily and effectively achieved by careful organization and structure on the part of the teacher.

In the light of the above assumptions I am tentatively advocating a schooling in which a fairly disciplined primary stage (with the exception of the 'exploring' aspect) gradually gives way to a less disciplined secondary stage. This may be contrasted with the prevailing fashion of trying to impose some sort of discipline on a free and open elementary stage. I should not have to add that by 'disciplined' I do not mean 'oppressive'. I mean rather that the teacher should organize class-time with a view to making progress with the task in question.

5.11 The above remarks fit uncomfortably alongside the apparent North American passion for quantification, systematization and the commitment to the ideology of "if it moves, measure it, and, if it doesn't, it can't be real". It seems appropriate therefore that I should at this point briefly make some observations and air some worries about such practices as teacher-evaluation, simulation games, values education, teaching objectives and models of teaching, all of which seem to be quite often talked about here and none of which have made much headway in Britain.

What, I wonder, occasions this passion for charts, diagrams, tables, questionnaires, calculi and quantification in general? Is this an example of the medium having become the message, so that it is assumed that, since the presentation looks scientific, what the charts and graphs depict must have a kind of reality and certainty that would otherwise not be apparent? Let us take, for example, the business of students being asked to fill out forms for an evaluation of the instructor. Asking people what they think of another person would seem on the face of it to be a paradigm example of an informal, unscientific and subjective procedure. But systematize that procedure a bit by drawing attention to what the group of persons asked has in common, by throwing in a bit of jargon so that the group becomes the 'sample', by putting the questions on paper (the 'questionnaire'), and finally, of course, by feeding the responses into the computer, and the operation begins to take on the appearance of being scientific and objective. So, in some sense and some respects, it is. But it is *not* the case that the verdict now delivered by the computer necessarily gives you a truer, more precise or more objective account of how the students reacted to you than did the informal approach, still less is it the case that it gives a truer more objective account of you as an instructor. What you get is some kind of an *objective calculation* of the material, but what was fed in was as subjective as ever. It may be averaged out more precisely, but that has nothing to do with whether it reflects any truth. It certainly may not reflect the truth; it may not even reflect the truth as seen by the class.

The problems and shortcomings in this kind of activity are obvious:

1) How does one know that what one person understands by key terms ('good', 'interesting', 'relevant') is what another person does?
2) How can one allow for the idiosyncracies of the individual respondent? (Some people are more easily interested than others.)
3) Often the questions asked are just inept in themselves. (These examples are taken from an evaluation sheet actually used at an Ontario college: "My instructor makes difficult topics easily understandable." (Then how do you know that they are difficult?) "My instructor easily builds rapport with the class." (So what?) "My instructor makes learning more interesting than I expected." (Doesn't that tell us rather more about you than about him?) "Students in this class are interested

in knowing each other" (for this I might get fired?). "This instructor has no peculiarities which I find distracting" (!))

4) If applied, in an institution, across a range of subjects, as they often are, such questionnaires make no allowance for inherent differences between subjects (e.g., in difficulty).
5) The whole question of the appropriateness of various questions needs to be examined. For example, is it appropriate to ask whether taking another course from this instructor would be enjoyable?

No doubt it is important for instructors to acquire feedback about their teaching, and no doubt other ways of obtaining such feedback are equally prone to inaccuracy and distortion. But the besetting sin of this kind of formal evaluation procedure, apart from the uses to which it is sometimes put, is that because of its appearance, because it probably emanates from some fancy sounding research and design department, because it is superintended by some statistics professor who needs to take himself seriously, it acquires a status that it in no way deserves. Just think of the different connotations that the phrases "collecting opinions" and "doing research" have, and yet, at least in this instance, there is no appreciable difference between the two. Our feedback is, in the nature of our task, always going to be hazy and inaccurate. Let us acknowledge the fact and not succumb to procedures that disguise it.

5.12 The question of appearances may also be raised in relation to such simple devices as flow charts and diagrams, which are particularly popular amongst writers on curriculum. I am not suggesting that such diagrams are necessarily useless nor denying that some people find them more readily comprehensible than others. But surely, given that we are a race of verbal thinkers and given that we communicate verbally, a diagram can only be understood ultimately in verbal terms. It certainly cannot tell us *more* than could be said in words, and for most of us most diagrams tell us considerably less. Take, for example, this simple model of curriculum design:

Aims and objectives
↓
Content
↓
Organization
↓
Evaluation

What on earth is the value of that? As it stands it is meaningless. To make it meaningful merely requires a few simple words, but if we have them at our disposal why resort to the diagram at all? As a matter of fact the above model represents a translation sometimes made of the four principal questions that Ralph Tyler enunciated as fundamental to curriculum planning:

1. What educational purposes should the school seek to attain?
2. What educational experiences can be provided that are likely to attain these purposes?
3. How can these educational experiences be effectively organized?
4. How can we determine whether these purposes are being attained?[14]

How much clearer are the questions. How much more subtle and precise too. And, as we have seen, some variant of them is needed anyway to explain the diagram. The more complicated the diagram the more it stands in need of explanation; so one cannot reasonably argue that if one is dealing with something far more complex than Tyler's four questions, a model will be correspondingly more useful. Even when the purpose of models is to simplify, they must increase in complexity as the things they model become more complex, if they are to be true to those originals. But once again my major fear is that the use of diagrams and charts in educational theory is effectively serving to give an appearance of 'hard research', 'factual relevance' and 'objectivity' to material that is very often devoid even of interest.

5.13 Values education programmes, at least as the phrase is generally used, consist essentially of stimuli (generally fictional stories involving apparent moral dilemmas) designed to cause the student to articulate his values. It is not inherent in most such programmes to probe for reasons that may lie behind the student's value position; still less is it an inherent part of most programmes to demand good and coherent reasoning on the matter or to improve the quality of the reasoning offered. For example, a story is told involving Heinz who faces the problem of whether or not to steal a drug, which is overpriced in the drug store and which he consequently cannot afford, in order to help his sick wife.[15] The student is specifically informed that "there are no 'right' answers in the way that there are right answers to mathematics problems," which is a trifle disingenuous to say the least: it is true, without question, that the answers to moral problems are not of the same logical kind as the answers to mathematics problems, and therefore the nature of 'right' answers will differ in each sphere. But most students will infer from the statement made that there are no right answers in the moral domain in the sense that it is all fundamentally a matter of subjective opinion. So much for the central problem of moral philosophy! The fact is that it may reasonably be argued that there *are* right answers even in the moral sphere. The student is asked to respond to the story, first merely by stating his opinion as to whether Heinz should steal the drug. He is then presented with twelve propositions relating to the story and asked to say of each one whether it is more or less important in relation to Heinz's decision, on a five point scale. Finally he is asked to select the four most important propositions and rank them in order of importance. The propositions listed after this particular story incidentally are rather a confused jumble. The question of whether it is "only natural for a loving husband to care so much for his wife that he'd steal," leaving aside the ambiguity of the expression "only natural," is of a quite different kind to the question of whether it should make a difference that Heinz would be acting for another rather than himself. The latter is at any rate a *moral* consideration; the former is not. Similarly the question of whether Heinz is "willing to risk getting shot as a burglar" has nothing to do with the moral side of things. (It is anyway more or less meaningless to ask in this context whether it is more or less important that he might be willing to risk getting shot.)

Of course, it might be argued that it makes a considerable difference how such tests and programmes are used. Certainly a good teacher might tell the Heinz story and weave the sort of questions noted and their answers into some kind of an intelligible and useful exercise. The point to stress is that in themselves these programmes appear to be clumsy and artificial ways of doing little more than asking students to state their opinions. The danger is that that exercise, which is probably harmless and might be invested with some sort of point, will be taken far more seriously than it deserves, because the tests used are the result of research, they are all systematized so that answers can be fed into the computer, and before long people will be assuming that it has something to do with moral education, which on the face of it, it certainly does not have. There is the added risk that the extensive use of such techniques in schools will encourage students to confuse a willingness to state one's opinions with rational autonomy.

The efficacy of values education programmes of this sort would seem to depend partly on the extent to which human nature is or is not malleable and developed by circumstance and environment. If individuals remain essentially what they are throughout life, a stronger case could be made for the use of values education, since there is at least some point in encouraging people to articulate and explain the views they will persist in holding. The more one believes in the notion of some kind of environmentally developed and changing human nature, the less reason there would seem to be to devote time to articulating present views rather than developing the moral self. The basic point is that though values education may be an innocent pastime it is no substitute for and no necessary part of moral education, being neither specifically moral (not all values are moral values) nor obviously educational. There are important differences between expressing, exploring, assessing and justifying moral values. Values education seems only concerned with the first of these, while moral education is intimately connected with the last three.

In just the same way it is difficult to see how such things as creativity tests, lateral-thinking games or even the semi-sacrosanct Watson-Glaser critical thinking tests are deemed to have any particularly significant use. Once again, there is no need to suggest that there is something inherently wrong with such tests; it is just that any useful purpose they might serve from an educational point of view is difficult to discern. What do they tell us beyond the fact that one is good or bad at doing the test in question? Nothing, because what the typical creativity test tests is not recognisable as some general characteristic such as the word 'creativity' normally refers to. Being good at thinking of uses for a brick is being good at thinking of uses for a brick.[16] It tells us nothing for certain about whether the student in question will be good at thinking of uses for an old skate, less still about whether he will be good at thinking of things to do in real life situations, and absolutely nothing about his creativity in the sense that Beethoven or Rembrandt could be said to be creative. Similarly, unless one defines critical thinking as the ability to do well on Watson-Glaser tests, the tests do not obviously tell one anything at all about critical thinking as popularly understood.

5.14 Contemplation of simulation games gives rise to the interesting question of whether it may not be that the only things they can actually teach are the things that are real and not simulated in the game. Take, for example, the political simulation game *Caucus*.[17] To play *Caucus* is certainly to acquire a lot of political information, but then the information given is real information which there are plenty of other ways of acquiring; by playing the game one may also learn things such as that sometimes one can negotiate changes with people, but that too is something that players really do in the game. (You don't simulate negotiation, you negotiate.) But the one thing that the game surely cannot give you is the sense of what it really is like to be a politician negotiating. In real life it just isn't the same thing as it is when playing *Caucus*. So what is it that we are supposed to learn by simulating it? And what do we learn here that couldn't be equally well learnt in many other ways? Since my purpose is not to say that such games are not worth playing, but to ask what benefits they have over other ways of teaching, I might add that teaching through a game such as *Caucus* would appear to be a relatively time consuming and inflexible method. (It may also be more fun, which could be a sufficient justification for some.)

5.15 It seems to me that the progressive tradition was right about one thing: we must resist methodological totalitarianism or the domination of particular teaching styles. The preoccupation with such tests and strategies as I have referred to (and I might have added others) approaches what I shall term a mechanistic totalitarianism, under which any teaching technique that involves measurement, systematization, quantification, or technological hardware is welcome and everything else is suspect.

What is fundamentally wrong with that is that it distorts education which surely is basically not a quantifiable activity. The behavioural objectives model of teaching, for example, I would suggest, unless very carefully used as a minimal part of the whole, is outrageously restrictive to the enterprise of true education. We should embrace unrealisable aims, not devise strategies to escape them, because education, like love, is at best about the unknown, the unclassified, the perfect. This is not a matter of being vague and woolly. It is a case of facing up to the fact that the concept of education is broad and idealistic, and that most ideals are difficult, if not impossible, to attain fully. If we scale the operation down to specify graspable objectives, we may gain a feeling of achievement, but we grasp minimal achievements. In the same way a married couple can live up to the attainable and testable objectives of a kiss in the morning, mouthing "I love you" and so on. That way the mechanistic-minded could keep an eye on 'love', as some professors of education are keeping the field of 'education' under control. But that way love, real love, is lost sight of. I have admitted throughout the above paragraphs that a lot depends upon how these various teaching techniques or strategies are used: they are not (most of them) inherently obnoxious. But the worry is that the sheer preponderance of such strategies and the emphasis on them in North American educational discourse will in themselves turn education into an industry to be assessed in terms of productivity, market research and profit.

5.16 It is appropriate that I should end these comments by reference to the models of teaching approach advocated by some for the initial preparation of teachers, since that will serve as a convenient link with the final chapter. The pedagogic convenience of a book such as Bruce Joyce's and Marsha Weil's *Models of Teaching* is beyond dispute.[18] There we find encapsulated accounts of the educational views of such diverse figures as Thelen, Bruner, Taba, Piaget and Skinner, and the whole makes a very useful reference book. But we should not delude ourselves about the nature of such a book: it is in effect the modern variant of what would have been called "Ideas of the Great Educators" twenty years ago. And it displays the same kinds of shortcomings, most particularly that of being remarkably uncritical. Up to a point that is deliberate. Joyce and Weil are anxious to stress that all of these models have their merit and it is not for them to tell students which is the best. That is very laudable, but to refuse to be dogmatic about the superiority of one teaching style is one thing; to introduce the ideas of Piaget, Skinner and Schutz as if there were no questions about the coherence, sense or quality of what they say is quite another. The disturbing element, in other words, is not the refusal to rank order the models, but the lack of critical onslaught on each individual model. This lack of concern for intellectual rigour also shows itself in the way that such disparate figures as Thelen and Skinner rub shoulders. After all, one of these is primarily concerned about finding means to promote democratic attitudes in people while the other concentrates on demonstrating the efficacy of classical, operant conditioning. But that these various models are often based on different kinds of theoretical bases, and therefore may need to be questioned in quite different kinds of ways, is something the student would not appreciate from this book alone.

Apart from the superficiality of the models, the major objection to this approach is the straight-jacketing that it inevitably imposes on our approach. That may seem unfair since Joyce and Weil do their best to stress that dogmatism about these models would be antithetical to them. But to say as they do that the student may want to employ a different model with a different class isn't good enough. Teaching just isn't like this: the good teacher does not select his programme as if he were a washing machine, not even had he twenty programmes to choose from. He may need to "change programmes", if we must talk in this way, every minute or with every child. It is not a question of there being a time for Piaget and a time for Plato. Piaget and Plato, or the valuable parts of what they have to say, need to be understood and internalized so that they become part of the teacher's thinking. Then the teacher must become himself all the time, responding not programmatically but directly to every changing nuance of the situation. Once again I am talking in ideal terms. So I should. Why sell ourselves and our children short?

What this boils down to, as Joyce is well aware, is the question of whether we accept the sort of major assumptions that he cites as lying behind teacher competency based programmes. "One was that the acts of teaching and the responses of the learner could be reasonably analyzed into specific, even minute, behavioural components without doing violence to the essential nature of the act. A second is that . . . teaching is not an intuitive art but is composed of discernible patterns of behaviour the dimensions of which can be productively changed through training."[19] (Note here the use of the technique of over-simple polarization.) My contention is that as I understand "the essential nature of the act" of teaching (with a view to *education*, rather than mere instruction or training) these assumptions are just false. Rather than design programmes based upon them, we should at most design programmes that provide opportunities to consider and discuss them.

Notes

1. *Basic Skills at School and Work*, op. cit., p. 110.
2. Ibid., p. 127.
3. Ontario Ministry of Education, *English Curriculum Guideline for the Intermediate Division*, 1977, p. 5.
4. Ibid., p. 3.
5. Ibid., pp. 7, 4.
6. I should add that, of course, I do not share the vocationally orientated view of education held by the commercial class of Albertown (*Basic Skills at School and Work*).
7. Non-rational rather than irrational. I take 'irrational' to refer to behaviour or argument based on bad and irrelevant reasons. The non-rational is outside the sphere of the rational. Thus one might say that love is generally non-rational rather than irrational. See R. G. Woods and R. Barrow, *An Introduction to the Philosophy of Education*, op. cit., ch. 5.
8. On the other hand, it should be cautioned that we have a minute body of successful television drama, it is not readily accessible to the student, and in some cases full appreciation would seem

to depend upon understanding that can only be achieved through prior reading of the novel.

9. Of course, it depends to some extent on how one defines geography and the Ministry guidelines do make it look rather all-embracing. See Ontario Ministry of Education *Geography Guideline for the Intermediate Division*, 1977.
10. Morley Callaghan quoted by Mordecai Richler, "Nationalism and Literature in Canada" in G. Milburn and J. Herbert (eds.), *National Consciousness and the Curriculum*, Toronto: O.I.S.E., 1974, p. 110.
11. Ontario Ministry of Education *History Guideline for the Intermediate Division*, 1977, p. 6.
12. Neville Bennett, *Teaching Styles and Pupil Progress*, London: Open Books Publishing Ltd., 1976.
13. See *Ethics and Education*, op. cit.
14. The example, diagram and list of Tyler's questions are all taken from Denis Lawton, *Social Change, Educational Theory and Curriculum Planning*, London: University of London Press, p. 13. However, I am not here trying to criticize Lawton's work.
15. What follows is taken from the unpublished questionnaire *Opinions about Social Problems*, prepared by James Rest, 1972.
16. The example is taken from a creativity test discussed in my *Moral Philosophy for Education*, op. cit., ch. 10.
17. *Caucus II: Canadian Politics in Action: A Simulation Game*, revised and expanded by G. Milburn and W. A. Houston, Toronto: Van Nostrand Reinhold, 1976.
18. Bruce Joyce and Marsha Weil, *Models of Teaching*, Englewood Cliffs, New Jersey: Prentice-Hall Inc., 1972.
19. Bruce Joyce *et al.*, *Preservice Teacher Education*, Palo Alto, California, 1977, p. 128.

CHAPTER 6

The Faculty of Education Curriculum

6.1 It has often been remarked that education faculties always seem to be situated "down the road". It is less often acknowledged that they are situated between the devil and the deep blue sea. Much of the rest of a typical university, perhaps anxious to locate a scapegoat, looks down on the education faculty as non-academic and non-scholarly. From that point of view education faculties are straight professional schools which make the strategic error of trying to offer academic courses that ape their counterparts in the university at large. On the other hand many teachers and Ministry officials object to education faculties on the grounds that they are too academic, too theoretical and—a word we shall hear more of—irrelevant.

Sometimes within the faculty itself there is a similar crude polarization so that foundations departments[1] seem more concerned to appear academically pure than to do anything else, and curriculum instruction departments feel a need to make snide and damaging remarks about the irrelevance of theory.

6.2 The situation in Ontario is not very dissimilar to that in Britain. But one or two differences should be noted at this point.

British university education faculties seem to be more sure of themselves and more securely part of the university as a whole. One may speculate on the reasons for this, but one pertinent factor must surely be that Britain, even with recent and current government reorganization, has a much larger and more solid system of colleges of education as distinct from university departments.[2] These colleges are not comparable to the old Ontario teacher colleges. The colleges of education in Britain *are* more or less as some people want to see Ontario faculties of education. That is to say, they are not in fact part of a university, although very often a university validates their courses. They are places which function in some respects like mini-universities, where people who couldn't or didn't go to university study for a degree and a teaching qualification over a three or four year period. Students with university degrees may also go to a college for one year to get a teaching qualification. The existence of such a network of colleges naturally takes a lot of flak away from the university departments. (At least it does amongst those who are aware of the differences!) At the same time the colleges are not harassed and threatened by other university departments.

Most university departments of education do also run a one year pre-service programme to qualify university graduates for teaching. But in the first place, as you will see, they are dealing with a selective intake; secondly a substantial amount of the work of the faculty will be in the field of graduate work and research—the sort of work that in Ontario seems to be largely concentrated at the Ontario Institute for Studies in Education. (There will also generally be some kind of in-service programme for which a diploma will be awarded, and which corresponds more or less with the M.Ed degree offered by some university faculties in Ontario.)

A second difference that may affect the quality of life in an education faculty is the fact that Ontario schools are less free than those in England. My experience is limited, but from what I see and hear Ontario teachers are (or feel they are) curtailed by the administration of the school, the Ministry, and the grade system in a way that must gradually wear out all but the most rebellious. Students in Britain are, of course, no less capable than those anywhere else of responding to some invigorating and challenging idea "Yes, but what's the point? We don't control the schools." Nonetheless, over there, there does seem to be some practical purpose in talking to students in terms of doing their own thing or even blowing the whole system to pieces. Over here, I have sometimes sensed that the complaint that our ideas are impractical has too much truth: the students will not be free to experiment with them.

6.3 It is also worth drawing attention to the American situation, since that is the subject of the most recent empirical research into teacher preparation.[3] According to that research the notion that concern for publication dominates faculty life is not borne out by any productivity statistics. "The average publication rate per person is about one article every three years."[4] So such problems as there may be in this area do not appear to be due to the fact of scholarly devotion detracting our attention from practical concerns. (In Britain the college set-up takes the emphasis off publication anyway, except for those engaged in research and higher degree teaching in the universities.) Undergraduate (or pre-service) teaching is regarded as the most important factor in promotion and tenure by both faculty and administration, and attention is accordingly directed to that for the most part. When it comes to undergraduate (pre-service) teaching the use of educational technologies is infrequent, which particularly worries the authors because, they argue, most technologies need constant use to be truly successful.[5] Though welcome to me (see above 5.10 ff.), this disdain for so-called educational technology is the more surprising in that a very wide variety of teaching strategies and devices are cavalierly thrown in under the heading, including use of video-tapes, micro-teaching, simulation, taxonomies of educational objectives and questioning strategies. A curious statistic to record is the observation that "Methods instructors are seen by 62.6% as best able to integrate their course content with experience in the schools."[6] How, one wonders, could it be otherwise? Methods instructors are supposed to be involved with experiences in the school; it is at least an open question, which will be addressed below, whether and if so in what way foundation instructors are. And how, one wonders, could such a question have been asked except by those who assume that everything that goes on in a faculty of education should be directly concerned with school experience and practice—rather as if instructors in engineering should be told to stick with building bridges and to leave the theoretical abstractions of physics alone? Also worth noting is that 92% of students claim to have been motivated primarily by a desire to work with children.[7] That is to be welcomed, no doubt. But note that, if that were in any significant number of cases also their only real motivation (which is not clear), it leaves a great deal for the pre-service programme to do. Everything, in fact, except dwell on the need for love and concern for children.

Implicit in both the preceding paragraph and the research to which I am referring is the very common assumption that teacher preparation needs some kind of overhaul. The most interesting statistic, therefore, is surely that which indicates that the satisfaction of students with their courses is very high. Do we then (or at any rate do the Americans) need to make any dramatic changes? Isn't this evidence that all is for the best and they should leave well alone? Possibly, but I am inclined to doubt it. First, in a general way, I question the reliability of responses to such questionnaires as are here involved. (May not many students, euphoric at the end of their courses, now qualified, be more benign in their judgement than they have at times felt?) Second, there is the question of whether their perceptions of what is a good or satisfactory course are reliable. Thirdly, there is the closely related question of whether we should assess our programmes by reference to student satisfaction. (At any rate, the view of the student ten years later might be more pertinent than his view now, before he has become a teacher in the full sense of the word.) For there is also to be considered the question of whether what is done makes sense and is the most rational kind of programme that could be adopted. It is this last question that I now wish to pursue—a question to which the use of questionnaires to arrive at generalizations about attitudes is wholly inappropriate.

6.4 On the face of it the current situation in much of Ontario is quite simply inadequate, since it is based on little more than the demand for a certain number of credits taken from practically any of a large number of disparate courses. It is what one might term the 'smorgasbord' approach, allowing considerable choice of courses both across and within subjects and disciplines. Thus a student might do three history courses or none; one student nominally doing philosophy may do a course on sex-roles, another a course in formal logic; a student's experience with one method tutor in social science may bear no relation to another student's with another tutor. What is the more reprehensible is that, besides very often the absence of any clear rationale for what is on offer and the openness of the offer, the student's choice is necessarily blind. Timetable problems, misleading course descriptions, inaccurate preconceptions, and ignorance all conspire to make the final programme of study more a matter of luck than good judgement. Whatever the truth about the American situation, it seems to me quite evident that Ontario at least is currently turning out far too many unwanted, inappropriately prepared and bewildered teachers who feel that their year of pre-service preparation was divided between Mickey Mouse courses and challenging but irrelevant courses. If there is any truth in such a picture, what is needed are not new strategies or new ways of teaching teachers or more relevant in the sense of more down to earth courses. Rather it is a question of pausing, taking time out and asking ourselves what sort of things we should try to do if we wish to prepare people for teaching. If we do that and then ask what the purpose of some of the current courses is supposed to be, we may find a disturbing lack of fit. (It may be that the preparation of elementary and high school teachers should differ in important ways. In the remainder of this essay I shall assume we are concerned with high school teachers.)

6.5 The primary task of a teacher preparation college (and I have a reason for using that phrase) is presumably to ensure that teachers are competent to carry out the schooling demands made on them. This surely means at least a) mastery of the subject matter to be taught, b) mastery of various ways of teaching different types of material to different individual students, and c) personification of the values that we hope to develop in children. (Not merely *moral* values.) As things are it seems that considerable concern is shown for a)—considerably more than is shown in Britain, for example. On the other hand, as indicated above, the students who enter the university departments in Britain are a more select group, and their first degrees are a better guide to their competency in this respect than a first degree would be in Canada. Very little concern seems to be shown for c) in either Britain or Canada. And yet this is of great importance. If we really believe in the power of the child's surroundings to influence, we should surely pay great attention to those surroundings, which of course include the characters of the teachers. If it is perhaps too late to create in the pre-service teacher such virtues as concern for others, concern for reason, concern for clarity and accuracy, honesty and reliability, it should at any rate be part of the teachers' college's function to consider and assess with reference to such qualities. Nominally b) is currently one of the pre-service programme's main interests. The question here is what the right way to go about mastering flexible teaching abilities may be. What is involved in the ability to teach well? Surely it is the ability to sense the appropriate moment for doing various different things. Since it involves this element of judgement as well as various techniques it cannot finally be reduced to the measurable and quantifiable. There is also an element of personality or character involved in the definition of the good teacher in its fullest sense, which is not to be reduced to behavioural ticks either. As I have tried to argue explicitly and implicitly throughout this essay, teaching is not an amalgamation of motor responses, models, techniques, skills and the use of audio-visual aids. Teaching is, if not an art, a talent that in its fullest flowering depends upon the intangibles of character and intellect, and in Alexander Pope's words, "Men must be *taught* as if you taught them *not*."[8] Consequently in the end the only place to learn to teach, to grow and improve as a teacher is on the job. As far as teaching well goes, though there may be a place for discussion and reflection arising out of practice, there is no necessity for such things as understanding Piaget, appreciation of the ideas of Rousseau, familiarity with the use of overhead projectors, carefully docketed models of teaching, carefully formulated lesson objectives or any of the rest of the rag-bag of educational hardware. There is reason to believe that without a thought for any of the above Socrates was a very great teacher. There is no reason to believe that even equipped with the above Thrasymachus would have been a good teacher.

What then are we to say of a fourth element, d) theoretical educational study, which as a matter of fact takes up most of the time available in the pre-service year? (I am classifying a good part of what goes on in curriculum and instruction courses as theoretical, as it seems to be in Ontario, as well as foundations courses. That is to say discussion of issues such as "Why teach history?", "What are social studies?", "How can one distinguish between good and bad literature?".) To that question I will devote some attention.

I understand the academic study of education to involve studying educational problems and issues in general rather than particular terms, abstractly rather than concretely, but not of course in isolation from such facts as there may be. In other words it is concerned with issues such as "What should the schools seek to do?" rather than "What is it best for the mathematics teacher to do with Johnny Smith this morning?". Fundamental to the study of any such general and abstract issues will be mastery of philosophy, psychology and sociology. In addition a strong, but slightly different, case can be made for history in this context. In order to substantiate this claim it is only necessary to consider the nature of these constituent disciplines.

6.6 Nowhere is there more misunderstanding amongst educationalists than there is over the nature of philosophy. This is perhaps not surprising, for it is arguable that there is a particular problem with philosophy in that, unlike psychology or history, it is the kind of activity that it is logically impossible to understand the significance, nature and point of without engaging in it, or at least without having been initiated into it rather than merely told about it. That is to say, whereas it is possible to explain the sort of thing that psychologists are up to (as one could explain to somebody what photographers or football players are up to, even if one was unfamiliar with those particular activities), explaining what philosophy is, is rather like explaining what an aesthetic sensibility is to someone who just doesn't have any kind of aesthetic reaction to things.[9]

Throughout a discussion such as this there is a danger of being hampered and plagued rather than helped by definitions. I must make it clear that boundary disputes are the last thing I want to encourage. Few things are more profitless than historians, psychologists and philosophers jealously guarding their territory and trying to define each other out of business. But what we do need is some understanding of different kinds of questions that might be and need to be asked, understanding of different kinds of activities as such, regardless of what they are best called or who does them.

As a matter of fact philosophy is not an unambiguous term

even amongst philosophers. French existentialists have a very different appearance to logical-positivists; German metaphysicians look uncomfortable in the same category as Oxford linguistic analysts. In my own case I find the North American preoccupation with formal logic courses and philosophy of science alien. Whereas to North Americans the British tradition that I represent is perhaps rather vague and casual. Nonetheless there is an important activity that we should be concerned with which would be recognized by most philosophers as essentially philosophical. I refer to examination of the meaning and logic of educational discourse. That activity is what I understand by the phrase 'philosophy of education'. The sort of thing it involves is best indicated by an illustration.

It has been said that "all knowledge is relative". In the end it may be that that is an empirical thesis (or set of empirical theses); certainly the view(s) represented by that statement is often expressed by sociologists who would claim to have empirical evidence that it is so. But caution is needed. That *what* is so? To be a philosopher means first and partly to have the kind of ears that prick up at neat sounding epigrammatic utterances such as this and won't let it pass unquestioned. On the face of it the remark is absurd, the philosopher might say, for what after all is knowledge? Surely by definition it is something like true belief backed by adequate evidence. Consequently strictly speaking one would have thought knowledge *could not* be relative—it is of what is, not of what seems to be.

Such a preliminary move in itself solves no deep problem. But it is important. Brief reflection on the meaning of 'knowledge' helps us see what we really need to inquire into: the meaning of 'relative'. Is there some special sense of 'relative' in which, notwithstanding what I've said about it, knowledge is relative, or will it turn out that what is meant is not that 'knowledge' but that 'what passes for knowledge' is relative?

In fact there are various possible theses that might be meant and that need to be distinguished here. Briefly:

1. What is regarded as true does vary from culture to culture.
2. Different things are true of different cultures.
3. There are identifiable groups in society that control what is regarded as true.

4. The types of truth that there are, are artificially categorized.
5. Nothing is true.
6. We can never be sure of the truth of anything.

Once broken down in this way, the matter immediately becomes less tense and less portentous. The first claim is obviously true and not threatening or even interesting; likewise the second. The fifth would be interesting if true, but it is patently absurd. The third probably contains much truth—and here further empirical research would be appropriate. The fourth is very complex and requires a lot more philosophical work. The sixth—well. . . .

Thus philosophy involves an attitude, the raising of certain questions, generally to the end of dissolving rather than solving problems. An essential part of solving real-world problems—but only a part. Because philosophy involves an attitude and technique rather than a body of information or data, it is something that the individual must have for himself. You cannot rely on others to do the philosophical work. Thinking well on any matter involves thinking philosophically. It has been said many times that we should hope for the day when there are no books on philosophy, but all books are philosophical. I endorse that view and it is because of the nature of philosophy that all education students ought to have to do it—assuming a case can be made for them studying education at all.

We should also, I suggested, be concerned with the logic of educational discourse. That is to say, when proposals are put forward or opposed, once we have an understanding of the central concepts, we should turn our attention to the coherence and consistency of the arguments produced. The study of formal logic, by the way, is neither necessary nor sufficient to that end. It is not a matter of studying or formulating rules of logic, but of examining the logic of actual arguments. One can do the latter without doing the former, because classifying and naming rules is distinct from recognizing an instance of a rule. One may appreciate that it is fallacious to deduce that children *ought* to study geography from the mere fact that at a given time and place they *do* study geography, without knowing that such argument is an instance of what has been termed the naturalistic fallacy. The important task for those interested in education is the former. It is therefore concern with logic in that sense that I have in mind as an essential part of the philosophy of education.

A negative point should now be clear: the study of philosophy of education thus defined is distinct from the study of educational ideas through the ages, although one might choose to examine such ideas philosophically (i.e., with a view to their meaning and logic). It should also be clear in what sense philosophy is particularly concerned with the area of value judgements and in what sense it is not. One does not have to examine the sphere of value judgements in education philosophically, nor does the study of philosophy lead to the automatic revelation of true values. The point is rather that since questions of value (What is good? What is best? What should we do?) cannot be solved by empirical research, we must try and arrive at a better understanding of the nature of those questions. How do value judgements function logically? What do they imply or mean? What kinds of criteria might count in deciding whether something is beautiful or just? Philosophy has been called a second-order discipline and that is correct, provided that 'second-order' is not misinterpreted to mean 'second rate' or 'of secondary importance'. It is second-order in the sense that it examines the basis of other disciplines by examining their fundamental concepts and procedures. Questions such as what constitutes objectivity in the social sciences or how coherent is the behaviourist theory of psychology are thus philosophical questions or (and this is the more important way of putting it) questions that are different in kind from the questions that the social scientist or behavioural psychologist seek to answer in their respective roles as social scientist and psychologist. Similarly it is for empirically-minded educationalists to carry out creativity or intelligence tests. But questions about what intelligence or creativity are (questions of meaning) and how to interpret the tests in a wider context (questions of the logic of the enterprise) are philosophical. Hence it has been rightly said that philosophy polices educational discourse.

Readers who are familiar with the work of Denis Lawton may recall a chapter in his *Class, Culture and Curriculum* where he says much the same sort of thing as I have said above about the relativity of knowledge.[10] Yet he is a curriculum expert, or perhaps a sociologist, rather than a philosopher. That is the reason that I used that particular example: he is technically, let us say, a sociologist. But when he pursues that kind of inquiry he is being philosophical. As I said above, it does not in itself matter who is called what or who does what. Indeed I hope it is true that very often psychologists, sociologists and historians indulge in what I have defined as philosophy. (It is the fact that Lawton does that makes his work admirable.) The only points that I am making are first that questions of the type "What might 'knowledge is relative' mean?" or "What is knowledge?" are distinct in kind from questions of the type "Is it true that knowledge is controlled in a specific way?", and secondly that they are crucially important, since until the former have been answered the latter cannot be examined.

Given the above points, a basic course in philosophy of education would consist in consideration of the meaning of some of the key concepts in the educational enterprise (e.g., education itself, knowledge, intelligence, creativity, critical thinking, interest and discipline) and the coherence of various claims and arguments made about or in relation to those concepts. (See Figure 2)

6.7 If it takes rather less space to outline the nature of the remaining disciplines, that is to be attributed not to any difference in importance but to the point made above about their different logical status. They are easier to explain or give an account of, if not to do. Psychology consists in the systematic study of human behaviour and motivation. There are of course many different schools of psychology, and different psychologists may be interested in different kinds of questions, conduct different types of inquiry and offer different types of explanation. The behaviourist, for example, is interested in explaining things in terms of observable behaviour, whereas other psychologists such as those of a Freudian persuasion may not be. Therefore one cannot briefly describe the procedure of psychology nor profitably list all the various procedures that might be involved, but one can reasonably characterize the discipline as the systematic study of human behaviour and motivation. It is then extremely important for our purposes to bear in mind the distinction between:

1) teaching psychology, which will involve studying some of the procedures with a view to seeing how certain

Argument: any soundly conceived educational proposal and any sound criticism of educational proposals or practice presupposes the avoidance of conceptual and logical confusion. The following introductory course is designed to promote a sensitivity to the danger of such confusion and to develop a competence in dealing with such confusion in this sphere of education. It is designed to help the student to police his own thought, the thought of the empirical disciplines, and the thought and practice of the school system.

Proposal: Course title: *Introduction to the philosophy of education*

Aim: to provide understanding of the philosophical method in relation to key educational issues.

1. The nature of philosophical inquiry: concern with meaning and the coherence of argument.
2. The central concept, 'education', is examined and compared with such related concepts as 'schooling'/'training'/'indoctrination'.
3. 'Knowledge' being closely associated with 'education', the nature of 'knowledge' is now examined. (This section could pursue many questions. It is important that reference should be made to the work of contemporary sociologists of education and the so-called sociology of knowledge.)
4. 'Intelligence' and such related concepts as 'creativity'/'critical thinking'/'rationality' are now examined and compared. (Here close reference should be made to the work of psychology of education.)
5. The problems inherent in the sphere of value judgements need to be outlined and considered in view of the extent to which value judgements play a part in education.

Figure 2. Specimen proposal for an introductory course in philosophy of education.

conclusions are arrived at and acquiring understanding of the procedures;

2) teaching psychological data, by which I mean informing people of the findings of certain psychologists, without attempting to provide understanding of the procedures that led to them;
3) teaching the philosophy of psychology, which would involve initiating students into the business of examining the logic and coherence of the procedures and basic psychological concepts themselves.

Thus, if we take as an example anxiety, a course designed with a view to teaching psychology will seek to provide students with understanding of the kind of questions about anxiety that interest psychologists and how they set about attempting to answer them. If the concern were rather to inform students of what kinds of situations have been shown to be anxiety-provoking and other similar matters, the course would have become one that would better be described as teaching psychological data. If the instructor begins to probe the question of what constitutes anxiety and to consider whether certain procedures can reasonably be thought to tell us anything about anxiety, he shifts his course to one in the philosophy of psychology. In practice there is no reason at all why a course should not seek to combine all three elements. But it is important to bear in mind that they are logically distinct, since we have to face the question of what exactly we should teach in an educational faculty. On the face of it only the second has any obvious and immediate bearing on teaching. But I will return to this matter below.

By sociology I understand the systematic study of human groups and group behaviour. Just as with psychology, there are a number of quite different procedures that different sociologists might adopt and a tripartite division can be made between teaching sociology, teaching sociological data and teaching the philosophy of sociology. That is also true of history, by which I mean the systematic study of the past in such a way as to seek to explain the occurrences and events of the past and present.[11] (It is, incidentally, very curious to me, coming from Britain where sociology currently dominates psychology in educational institutions, to see that in Ontario sociology of education scarcely exists as an independent discipline. Furthermore it does seem a good example of the institutional control of knowledge, for to provide courses in psychology and not in sociology is implicitly to make certain suggestions about the kinds of factors that determine events in education. Suggestions that are, to say the least, highly questionable.)

The contribution that history may make is less direct and more contingent than that of psychology or sociology, but none the less significant for that. The latter two disciplines provide data that is itself the data of the educational enterprise. The contribution of history is indirect in that we can gain in understanding or learn from experience through history. But the fact remains that, logically, educational planning without reference to psychological or sociological data is planning in ignorance of the facts of the matter in hand. That is not so of educational planning without reference to history, which would be unwise rather than nonsensical.

6.8 Such, in brief, I take to be the nature of the constituent disciplines of education. What I understand by the academic study of education is the study of these four disciplines in some way or other. The question that is most often asked about them either individually or together is whether they are relevant, which is also one of the most foolish questions that could be asked when presented without qualification in that way. Relevant to whom and to what and for what purpose? Of course they have relevance to some people for some purposes. What doesn't? The important question is not the meaningless "Are they relevant?" but the fundamental "What are we trying to do? What purpose are we trying to serve in faculties of education?" It is for example self-evident, given what I have said about them, given their nature, that these four disciplines are relevant to informed educational opinion and the study of education. They constitute the latter and educational opinion cannot be described as 'informed', if it is not based on understanding of both the facts of the matter and the procedures that were relied upon to locate them.

On the other hand it is highly debatable whether the study of these disciplines is directly relevant to the business of classroom practice. The findings of the disciplines may well have a bearing on classroom practice, though even here their significance tends to be overplayed: anything certain the psychologist or sociologist could tell the prospective teacher of a particular grade is either going to be trite or so hedged about with qualifications as to be vacuous. (If that is not so, it ought to be. We know so little for certain, and people as individuals are so unamenable to exhaustive scientific explanation, that there is very little one can say by way of abstraction and generalization that is both true and helpful for the newcomer to the classroom.)

The study of the disciplines themselves (as opposed to imbibing their findings) has no necessary connection with classroom teaching. Certainly there may be, contingently, some connection. A teacher, for example, might, as a result of beginning to study philosophy, think about the distinction between indoctrination and teaching. He might further come to regard his practice as indoctrination rather than teaching and consequently seek to change it. Or he might, as a result of studying Piaget, classify a particular child as being at a particular stage and modify his teaching accordingly. In this latter case, however, he did not need to study Piaget; at best he merely needed to learn the Piagetan stages by rote. In fact he didn't need to know anything about Piaget. It is quite possible to recognize that a particular child does not appear to be ready for or capable of a particular activity, without having a framework into which to fit that individual perception.

6.9 The question that is being forced upon us is: What are we trying to do in faculties of education? Above I used the phrase "teacher preparation colleges" deliberately, because I take it that as things are one thing that faculties are trying to do is prepare people to teach. The concept of teaching may be broad or narrow. For the moment I shall take it in the narrow sense to refer to classroom practice. Very clearly, if we are trying to prepare people for the particular job of classroom teaching, it would be appropriate to give them practice and one or two tips culled from experience. In addition it would be appropriate to give them all relevant legal information, understanding of the economic dimension to schooling and an appreciation of the nature and problems of administration. I say 'appropriate' because even with these down to earth matters, there is no obvious *necessity* to make prospective teachers become involved. Knowledge of the law is seldom going to effect one's practice, and when it does become pertinent one can always find out about the legal situation. Economic factors certainly effect schooling policy, but they need not touch the individual teacher. All one can say is that, if we decide to concentrate on equipping teachers with the nuts and bolts of their trade, it is here rather than amongst foundations courses that we should be looking.

Where does this leave the foundations disciplines? Arguably, without an immediate role. Arguably, while preparing people to teach is the wrong time to require them to study education. But at any rate let us stress that that is what these disciplines are relevant to: the study of education. What this means is that to justify the foundations disciplines in a teacher preparation course we must insert a premiss—and we must believe in that premiss and be prepared to argue for it when challenged. That premiss is that a teacher should be more than a trained instructor—more that is to say than one skilled in getting a specifiable content learned. He should himself be an educated man, which I take to mean a man of wide understanding and culturally developed. Specifically he should have thought long, hard and seriously about education—about what is possible, what is fair, appropriate and just.[12]

Many reasons might be advanced to support this demand. But for the moment I am content to leave it with the mere assertion that entrusting our children, our future, to a profession is quite sufficient reason for making strong demands on the members of that profession.

Once it is clear that the reason for getting people to study history, psychology, sociology and philosophy of education is so that they can think intelligently about educational matters, the question of relevance can be dismissed as what it is: a confusion. Of course these disciplines are relevant to such thought—they constitute it. The only question is whether teachers should think intelligently about such things. Who dares challenge that they should?[13]

6.10 The organization of such a course of study is a further matter. It is the case that the ultimate aim is that students shall be able to synthesize and bring to bear the expertise they gain in the various disciplines on educational issues and topics. It does not however follow as a matter of logical necessity that they should study the disciplines as part of some integrated course. There are a variety of options: one might begin by focussing on some educational issues, note how they give rise to different kinds of questions and subsequently pursue these distinct questions into the realm of the various disciplines. One might integrate all the disciplines around particular topics throughout the course. One might begin by initiating the student into each discipline independently and then require him to address himself to complex educational problems. One might stop short at introductory courses in the disciplines and leave the student to effect his own synthesis. But in fact, though this issue of how to organize foundations is often the most widely discussed, it seems to me a matter of very little moment and one which should anyway be decided by the exigencies of each particular situation. (Don't, for instance, demand integration from a group of unfriendly people.) All that matters (but this does matter very much) is that by the end of the course the student should recognize as distinct the distinct disciplines and move about in each one confidently and capably, should have the ability to recognize the logically distinct dimensions to complex problems, and should have the ability to synthesize these different dimensions in coping with the problem as such. That being the objective, each discipline should be primarily concerned to create a solid introductory programme that both initiates the student into the discipline and addresses itself to central educational issues. The smorgasbord offerings, referred to above, should be taken away. A course on, say, the history of education in Ontario since the war, a course on measurement and evaluation, and a course on the philosophy of science do not add up to the study of education.

6.11 The remaining question is when should this study of education take place? I said earlier that it might be that ideally it should not take place in the pre-service year. A strong case could be made for the view that what is needed in that year is an unashamed and effective programme of training. In my view there is also a strong argument for basing the year's work more on an apprenticeship system that takes its beginning from the school itself. In other words the student would be apprenticed to an experienced teacher who remains in the schools but who has an interest in teacher-training. (He would be the equivalent of the current curriculum and instruction professor in the faculty of education.) That tutor would be expected also to discuss the nature and problems of teaching and to cover the nuts and bolts material referred to above. On this model there would therefore be no teacher preparation colleges. But there would be university faculties of education. When people are no longer beset by fear of teaching or exhausted by years of undergraduate study, and when there are no confusions or illusions about the nature of the enterprise, the faculties of education would offer them something that would be salutary for the profession anyway: a sabbatical year to think about what the profession is up to as a whole, for the academic study of education. Preferably this would not be geared to any promotion or increase in salary, but it would be obligatory.

If the above seems too idealistic, then for the present let us try to do everything within the existing faculties of education. But if we do do that, let us draw attention to the clear differences between various activities we superintend. In particular let us cease to pretend that the justification for making students study foundations courses has much to do with improved classroom practice, and, conversely, let us cease to intellectualize the business of helping people take their first steps as practising teachers.

6.12 What in short I am asking for is that members of the teaching profession should first of all be unashamedly trained, but should then ideally become 'educated men' rather in the mould of Renaissance man. That is to say, they should have an educated view—in the liberal-education tradition—of education. They should be what so many of us are not: educationalists. They should have rounded intellects with knowledge and understanding of the history of education, the data of the empirical sciences and the approach and methods of philosophy. Some, I know, fear that to advocate educationalists—indeed to stress education rather than the present disciplines of 'history', 'philosophy' or whatever—is to threaten our purity, to weaken our competence. There is no necessary reason why that should be so. I am not advocating any watering down of anybody's competence—not asking for or expecting any of us to be less a philosopher, historian or whatever. But we are supposed to be historians of *education*, philosophers of *education* and it seems to me right and proper that we should put that up front. It is our job to *make* the study of education academically respectable and to *create* pride in our work. We have a far more honourable task ahead of us than tagging on to the coattails of a parent discipline.

But education is a field for multi-disciplinary inquiry; it is therefore in the end reprehensible to stand in the way of anything that seeks to allow and encourage future generations to bring these disciplines together or to make the synthesis that many of us are incapable of making. We have to think here —as all teachers have to—of the majority. One or two very able students, perhaps, want, deserve and should be encouraged to do historical research in depth: but that is to start talking about something else. I am addressing myself to the question of what we should offer to all teachers. And the answer is competence in educational discourse—not merely in one contributory discipline.

In the final analysis, the most outrageous thing about the present situation is that our teachers are themselves ill-educated and ill-equipped to reflect rationally on education.

It is my hope that the present essay has provided something upon which people may reflect—a base from which the task of thinking things through may begin.

Notes

1. In some faculties foundations departments are actually called academic departments.
2. Another factor may be the relatively small size of British universities.
3. *Preservice Teacher Education*, op. cit.
4. Ibid., p. 3.
5. Ibid., p. 33.
6. Ibid., p. 52.
7. Ibid., p. 67 Table 4.28.
8. Alexander Pope, "An Essay on Criticism" in J. Butt (ed.) *The Poems of Alexander Pope*, New Haven: Yale University Press, 1963, p. 162, line 574. (Emphasis added.)
9. For further discussion of the logical status of philosophy see J. P. White, *Towards a Compulsory Curriculum*, London: Routledge and Kegan Paul, 1973, and my *Common Sense and the Curriculum*, op. cit.
10. Denis Lawton, *Class, Culture and Curriculum*, op. cit.
11. It is important to draw a distinction between history and historicism. For most of us there is a clear distinction to be

drawn between explanation and justification. To say how something came about is not the same thing as saying that it should have done, or that it is good that it did. Indeed, there is a name for the fallacious confusion of the two: the naturalistic fallacy. It is no part of history qua history to say anything about the justification of events and actions in its purview, although of course historians as individuals may often wish to go into that. But there is one school of history that runs the two together by denying the existence of a separate realm of questions of justification. And this is historicism.

What I mean by an historicist is one who believes that the historian can uncover certain inevitable laws that determine the course of history. Thus, to show it came about is one and the same thing as to show that it was inevitable that it should. If that were so the question of justification would indeed be otiose. But since no convincing reason has ever been given for assuming it to be so, we can safely ignore it.

Historicism, incidentally, despite its name is not exclusive to the area of history; sociologists and psychologists too may practise an exactly similar determinism which seeks to deny anything beyond the causal laws it unfolds.

12. I am not suggesting that this should be a criterion of the definition of 'the educated man'.
13. If one wanted to be difficult and upset people, one could argue that what matters is not actually *doing* psychology and sociology, but having access to their findings and having the philosophic competence to police their activities. One could say that history, though often illuminating is in fact dispensable, on the grounds that how things came about has no *logical* bearing on whether they should continue to be or on how to make them continue or change. One could say in short that informed thought about education requires, as informed thought in any sphere does, critical examination of the coherence of the argument for certain conclusions coupled with the intelligent synthesis of such conclusions—the second order, philosophical activity. To be an historian, psychologist or sociologist and to lack philosophic competence is to be useless and dangerous. Whereas the philosopher without facts just bides his time. One could say the value of the three lies in what they tell us and that can be digested in sources—whereas the value of philosophy is in a way of proceeding and that has to be understood by the individual. I can draw on your findings. You cannot draw on my expertise.

    But I have no desire to cause trouble; and in any case, as I say in the text, I think that a strong case can be made for saying that all teachers should study all four disciplines.

Notes

Notes

Announcing a complementary publication:

Faculty of Education Tape Series
Conversations with Educators

A CONVERSATION WITH ROBIN BARROW

This thirty minute discussion (available either on audio-tape or video-tape), highlighting Barrow's conception of the purposes and content of a common core curriculum, is a useful supplement to **The Canadian Curriculum: A Personal View**

Interviewer: John McPeck

Other tapes available in the same series:

A Conversation with Bruce Joyce (interviewer—G. Milburn)
A Conversation with Denis Lawton (interviewer—R. J. Clark)

Order Form

To: Publications Office, Faculty of Education, The University of Western Ontario, 1137 Western Road, London, Ontario, N6G 1G7

Your Name ______________________________

Your Address ____________ , ____________ **Code** ________

Please indicate with an X the tape(s) you require:

Conversations Series	Audio-Tape	Television Video-Tape	
	($5.00)	½" ($30.00)	¾" ($30.00)
BARROW			
JOYCE			
LAWTON			

Your Total Order: $ ________

All orders must be prepaid
Make cheques payable to "The University of Western Ontario"

Other titles of interest:

STARTING THE ARK IN THE DARK: TEACHING CANADIAN LITERATURE IN HIGH SCHOOL
Ian Underhill
1977 ISBN 0-920354-00-9 paperback only

THE COUNTRY OF THE YOUNG: UNITS IN CANADIAN LITERATURE FOR ELEMENTARY AND SECONDARY SCHOOL
Don Gutteridge
1978 ISBN 0-920354-02-5 paperback only

Additional details from
PUBLICATIONS OFFICE
Faculty of Education
University of Western Ontario
1137 Western Road
London, Ontario, Canada
N6G 1G7